hotels • restaurants • spas • shops

hongkongchic

hotels • restaurants • spas • shops

hongkongchic

To obtain preferential rates and amenities at the hotels
featured in *Hongkong Chic*, please register online at:
www.thechicseries.com
info@thechicseries.com

hotels • restaurants • spas • shops

hongkongchic

text sofia a. suárez • zoë jaques

·K·U·P·E·R·A·R·D·

executive editor
melisa teo

editors
candice lim • joanna greenfield

designers
annie teo • felicia wong

production manager
sin kam cheong

designed and produced by
editions didier millet pte ltd
121 telok ayer street, #03-01
singapore 068590
email: edm@edmbooks.com.sg
website: www.edmbooks.com

first published in great britain 2007 by
kuperard
59 hutton grove, london n12 8ds
telephone : +44 (0) 20 8446 2440
facsimile : +44 (0) 20 8446 2441
enquiries : sales@kuperard.co.uk
website   : www.kuperard.co.uk

Kuperard is an imprint of Bravo Ltd.

©2006 editions didier millet pte ltd

Printed in Singapore

isbn-10: 1-85733-414-0
isbn-13: 978-1-85733-414-2

COVER CAPTIONS:

1: The chic CD bar at Lane Crawford ifc mall.
2: A delicate dragonfly resting on a fence.
3: Reflection of an old public housing estate.
4: A rock concert.
5: Details of an exhibit.
6: A stunning showroom at OVO.
7: Vivid colours of Shanghai Tang's products.
8: The fiercely competitive dragon boat race.
9: The ice fountain in the Finnish sauna at the
Four Seasons Hotel Hong Kong.
10: Racing up the bun tower at the Cheung
Chau Bun Festival.
11: Pulsating neon lights of the city.
12: Siew mai in a bamboo steamer.
13: Night lights in Hong Kong.
14: The bar at Felix.
15: The famous view from The Peak.
16: A lamp at The Peninsula Spa by ESPA.
17: Disneyland has come to Hong Kong.
18: Joyce Fashion Show.
19: Kou, a showpiece home of pure indulgence.
20: Furniture detail at a boutique.
21: The legendary Kung Fu master Bruce Lee.

PAGE 2: The panaromic view of Hong Kong
Island from Felix's floor-to-ceiling windows.

PAGE 4: The geometric shapes of City Hall.

THIS PAGE: The sultry gaze of a photo mdoel.

PAGE 6: Hong Kong's hilly landscape by twilight.

PAGE 8–9: From its urban forest of buildings to
the boats in its harbours, Hong Kong is a city
where the old is constantly juxtaposed with
the new.

contents

hongkong+surroundings

hongkongbychapter

Deep Bay

Tuen Mu

Urmston Road

Lung Kwu Chau

Castl Peak Bay

The Broth

Chek Lap Kok

Hong Kong International Airport

Tung Chung

Lantau Islan

Shek Pik Reservoir

Shek Pik

Lantau Channel

Soko Islands

Around Kowloon

Hong Kong Island

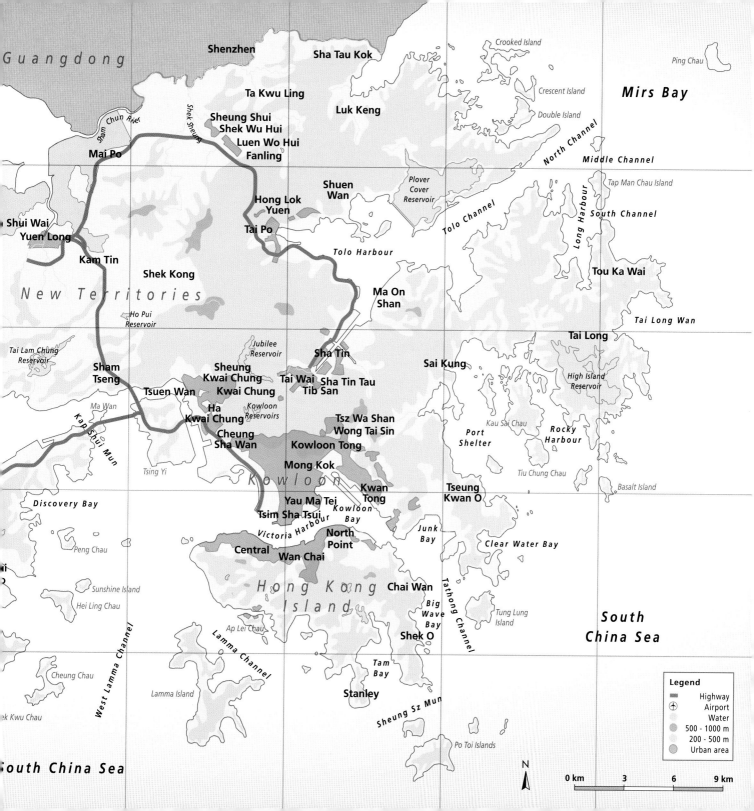

introduction

Gleaming skyscrapers, vivid explosions of fireworks and bustling, sign-filled streets—the glamorous postcard images of Hong Kong are only part of the story. It's the people who wrote it that make this exciting city utterly fascinating.

Almost 7 million people live, work and play in this former British colony. To be exact, the territory has a total area of 1,104 sq km (426 sq miles) and comprises four main areas: Hong Kong Island, the Kowloon peninsula, the New Territories, and 235 outlying islands. It sounds expansive; but about 70 per cent of the total area, surprisingly, still remains remote and rural.

Hong Kong enjoys one of the highest purchasing powers per capita in Asia, and its people love to amass and spend money. Gambling for fun and shopping for style, their conspicuous consumption is ultimately a matter of 'saving face' in this elegantly turned out and materialistic society. Yet at the heart of Hong Kong, life is centred on a Confucian sense of family, and multiple generations who live and eat together every day.

As the fourth most expensive city in the world to live in, Hong Kong's rents are sky-high and about one-third of its people rely on public housing. It is in these cramped conditions that Hong Kongers have developed and maintained the world's freest economy, sixth largest foreign exchange market, 11th largest trading economy, 13th largest banking centre, and Asia's second biggest stock market. So you'll have to excuse them if they seem a little rushed, or even rude. For hardworking Hong Kongers, time and space are money. In an ever-evolving city where the population has changed almost as often as the permanently under-construction skyline, it's essential to keep up with the pace or risk falling out of step.

Entrepreneurial and adaptable by necessity, Hong Kongers have weathered social, political and economic transformations in a short time span and have lived to tell the tale in several languages. Just look at businessman Li Ka-shing: the high school dropout is now the richest man in Asia, also ranking 10th on *Forbes'* 'World's Billionaires' list for 2006. His empire encompasses conglomerates Cheung Kong (Holdings) Limited

THIS PAGE (FROM TOP):
Bright neon signs reflect the city's electic atmosphere; people are constantly on the go, whether to play, eat or shop.
OPPOSITE: The celebrated view from The Peak is instantly recognisable and more stunning at night .

and Hutchison Whampoa Limited, and spans a world of industries—real estate, construction, banking, retail, Internet, telecommunications, electricity, transport, shipping, and more. The tiny territory has a total of 17 billionaires on that list.

Ambition characterises humble Hong Kongers too. They love to travel and take evening courses for self-improvement; and many of the highly educated people speak both official languages Cantonese and English, as well as Mandarin. English is widely used in business, government, legal and service sectors.

About 95 per cent of Hong Kong are of Chinese descent. The rest come from across the globe with the Philippines, Indonesia and the US topping the list, not to mention the South Asians, British and other nationalities who have been so closely linked to Hong Kong's growth. For over a hundred years, these diverse cultures have lived side-by-side; creating an identity that is unique to Hong Kong.

a 'barren rock'

Drug smuggling, disease outbreaks and several wars have coloured Hong Kong's vibrant history. Through it all, this little territory has persevered with a dogged determination to overcome an endless barrage of challenges and demonstrated an uncanny ability to adapt. Inextricably linked to Mainland China—physically, historically and economically—Hong Kong's amazing path parallels that of its big brother to the north; yet it remains defiantly unique. Hong Kong's history is also a tale of economic triumph on a 'barren rock' that began with no natural resources and few residents.

Hong Kong did not rise up out of the sea the day the British arrived. It is believed that the earliest settlements in Hong Kong date back to Neolithic times, as evidenced by bronze and stone tools, pottery and bronzes discovered on more than 20 sites

THIS PAGE: *Talented local designers showcase their work.*

OPPOSITE (FROM LEFT): *Hong Kongers dress up, whether it's formal couture or fanciful costumes; the spectacular exterior of the Louis Vuitton boutique at The Landmark, Central.*

across the territory. The earliest settlements in Hong Kong are believed to have been established by modern peoples from northern China around 2000 BCE; and Cantonese settlers from southern China arrived around 100 BCE. Prior to the arrival of the British in the 19th century, Hong Kong Island was composed of small coastal fishing villages, and was also known as a pirate's hideaway.

sung heroes

The most quoted pre-colonial tale is that of the ill-fated Southern Sung Dynasty (1127–1279) child emperor Zhao Shi and his younger brother Zhao Bing who fled from Kublai Khan's Mongol invasion of southern China to Lantau island in the late 13th century. After the elder boy died of illness, the younger brother succeeded as the last Sung emperor. His court moved to Sacred Hill above Kowloon Bay and resided near a large boulder until he died. The stone became known as Sung Wong Toi (as inscribed on its surface) or Terrace of the Sung Kings. During World War II, it was dislodged by the Japanese, but a portion of the stone bearing the original inscription survived and was cut into a tablet, then moved to a park specially built for it called Sung Wong Toi Garden. Legend also has it that the younger Sung emperor gave rise to the name Kowloon. There are eight mountains around the area that is today's Kowloon, and it was believed that a dragon resided in every mountain. Since emperors were also revered as dragons, so the place became known as Kowloon or gau long ('nine dragons') in Cantonese.

the british are coming

Europeans first began travelling to China to trade for silk, tea, porcelains and other exotic artefacts in the early 16th century. In 1557, the Portuguese settled in Macau, about 60 km (37 miles) to the west of Hong Kong, after a failed attempt to claim a strong-hold in Tuen Mun (now a district of the New Territories). Other Europeans

followed to stake their claims in the only authorised Chinese trading port at Canton (Guangzhou), up the Pearl River from Hong Kong. The British set up a trading port there in 1711; needless to say, they did not receive the red carpet treatment. Ching Dynasty (1644–1912) rulers saw non-Chinese people as barbarians, and announced a ban that imposed stringent restrictions on foreign traders. For instance, foreign warehouses were permitted only outside the city walls and closely monitored by Chinese officials. The British were further frustrated by a trade imbalance between the two countries, which was putting a strain on the royal treasury. So the British came up with a solution to

THIS PAGE: The harbour, chosen for trade, continues to convey countless container ships daily.

OPPOSITE (FROM LEFT): An aerial view of modern Kowloon; the name Kowloon or gau long translates to 'nine dragons' in Cantonese.

import vast quantities of something they knew the Chinese would grow to need: opium from Bengal. Until then, opium had been used for medicinal purposes, though its recreational uses were also known. The plan had its desired, ruinous effect. Drug addiction amongst China's population became so severe that in 1729 the Chinese placed a ban on imports of opium. However, like narcotics today, the profitable drug trade found ways around the laws, further filling the pockets of corrupt Chinese officials, British traders and pirates. By the 1830s, imports were up to 40,000 chests annually.

war on drugs

Antagonism over the continued illegal import of the 'foreign mud' culminated in the first Opium War (1839–1842). To protect their interests, now spread throughout East Asia, the British reinforced their navy and overpowered the Chinese forces. In January 1841, Captain Charles Elliot seized Hong Kong Island. His superiors were furious that he had chosen a 'barren rock' lacking both fresh water and fertile soil. They would have preferred one of the larger, more strategically placed islands to the north, right at the mouth of the Yangtze river.

However, the secluded location proved to be an asset. The harbour's great depth made it ideal for anchoring cargo ships; it was suitably situated on the main trading routes and offered entrances to the east and the west, and it provided a safe haven from attack and the climate's tropical storms. In August 1842, the Treaty of Nanking officially ceded Hong Kong as a crown colony to the British. Furthermore, five ports were opened to trade with the British, including key entrepôts Canton and Shanghai.

we are the world

At the birth of the colonial era, Hong Kong's minuscule population only numbered in the thousands but quickly grew. This was the time of the tai-pans (foreign businessmen in China or Hong Kong in the 19th century), as so glamorously depicted in James Clavell's novel. These fortune hunters were behind some of Hong Kong's oldest

THIS PAGE: The traditional Chinese junk, one of a dying breed that once filled the harbour.

OPPOSITE: A bird's eye view of Hong Kong's densely packed skyscrapers.

Today, about one third of Hong Kong's population lives in subsidised housing.

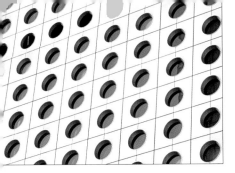

THIS PAGE (FROM TOP): *The iconic circular windows of Jardine House in Central; just steps away from modern skyscrapers, bustling street markets are full of character and eager bargain hunters.*

OPPOSITE: *Holding up a mirror to the past, the architectures of today come face-to-face with the artefacts of yesterday.*

business institutions, including Jardine Matheson & Co., from which the multinational corporation was created. In 1832, less than two years before the powerful East India Company was dissolved, Dr William Jardine and James Matheson founded a trading company in Canton. The head office was later established in Hong Kong in 1842.

As British officials, merchants and opium dealers settled on the island, they were followed by a wave of opportunity-seeking immigrants from China and other parts of the world—a recurring theme in Hong Kong's history.

South Asians, one of the territory's largest minority groups, were present early on as members of the British forces. Sikhs continued to hold high positions in the Hong Kong police force throughout British rule.

growing pains

Over the next half a century, the physical size of the colony grew exponentially. Victory in the Second Opium War (1856–1860) won the British 8 sq km (3 sq miles) of the Kowloon peninsula as agreed in the Convention of Peking (1860). Their biggest acquisition came after the Sino-Japanese war in 1898, when the New Territories in the north of Kowloon and 235 islands became part of the British territory under a 99-year lease that expired on June 30, 1997.

Population growth throughout the late 1890s was a strain on the newly formed communities. An epidemic of bubonic plaque ravaged Guangzhou and quickly spread to Hong Kong, claiming many lives daily. The horrific outbreak was also detrimental to trade, as the less devastating SARS (Severe Acute Respiratory Syndrome) crisis would also prove to be, more than 100 years later.

in and out

Hong Kong continued to be affected by skirmishes in Mainland China in the 20th century. Riots in the 1920s—following the end of the Ching Dynasty and the establishment of Sun Yat-sen's Republic of China in 1912—brought a flood of refugees that would again stress Hong Kong's population until the 1930s. In the meantime, economic rival Shanghai thrived as foreigners chose to invest in the 'Paris of the East'. Another wave of refugees poured across the border when Japan invaded China in 1938. By 1941, the population had swelled to 1.6 million. In December of that same year, the British surrendered Hong Kong to Japan following a bomb attack. The direction of migration changed and many escaped back to China. Those years of occupation were characterised by hardship, hyperinflation and food rationing. By 1945, the population had shrunk to 650,000.

Following the end of World War II, the British regained Hong Kong and sought to rebuild the economy. After the Communist regime was established in Mainland China in 1949, about 1 million people escaped to Hong Kong. Refugee camps were set up to accommodate them, but there were serious health and fire hazards. The government responded by developing public housing. Today, about one third of Hong Kong's population lives in subsidised housing.

karma chameleons

The territory's unrelenting adaptability was highlighted during the Korean War (1950–1953), when a United Nations trade embargo on China in 1951 dealt a blow to Hong Kong's economy. Its entrepreneurial residents responded by developing a manufacturing industry, which provided the basis for further industrialisation; it would employ half the workforce and contribute to about one-quarter of the territory's GDP within a decade.

Major exports were textiles, plastic toys, flowers, shoes, T-shirts, handbags and watches for the European and US markets. However, the industry relied on cheap labour working under harsh conditions. In 1967, the Cultural Revolution sparked labour disputes and political riots in Hong Kong. The situation was soon stabilised however, helped along by improvements in working and living conditions, and public works. In the 1970s, more subsidies were granted to educate the population. The country parks system was instituted. The Independent Commission Against Corruption was founded, helping to establish Hong Kong as one of the least corrupt societies in the world.

evolution to evolution

Instability in Mainland China in the 1970s brought foreign investments otherwise destined for Shanghai to Hong Kong and Singapore, and the economy boomed. To the credit of the British government, Hong Kong developed into a shining example of laissez-faire economics (Hong Kong has consistently topped the Index of Economic Freedom produced by the Heritage Foundation in collaboration with the *Wall Street Journal*). It created one of the world's leading stock exchanges (albeit temporarily dampened by a market crash in 1973). In addition to manufacturing, Hong Kong was also distinguishing itself as a centre for investment banking, fund management, venture capital and, of course, trade, boasting low taxes and access to markets around the globe. This evolution and diversification prepared Hong Kong to a degree for a new threat from an old rival in the 1980s: China's increasing openness and cheap labour costs made it a fierce manufacturing competitor.

lost in translation

In 1982, British Prime Minister Margaret Thatcher misread Deng Xiaoping's economic reforms and hoped for a continuation of the 99-year lease on the New Territories. Not only did China reject the idea; they refused to recognise any of the treaties, which they believed to be unfair and unequal, and demanded the return of the entire territory.

THIS PAGE (FROM TOP): Mao memorabilia in a street stall; the financial heart of the city, the Hong Kong Stock Exchange.

OPPOSITE (FROM LEFT): Koala shapes climb up Lippo Centre's twin towers, next to the golden Far East Finance Centre; imperial door wardens of ancient China, the guardian lion finds new relevance today guarding the city's riches.

...it was proposed that Hong Kong would be a Special Administrative Region (SAR)...

Deng, a forward-thinking reformer, recognised that Hong Kong's free market economy could not be assimilated into China's economic system overnight. In the Joint Declaration of 1984, it was proposed that Hong Kong would be a Special Administrative Region (SAR) based on a policy of 'one country, two systems'. Under those terms, it would be self-governing with its own currency, taxes, elected legislature (though vaguely stated) and the freedoms of speech, press, assembly, religion, and access to courts. Questions over the fate of the world's premier laissez-faire economy led to panic in the markets and Hong Kong's first big emigration.

on the move

On June 4, 1989, Hong Kong watched with personal interest as the Tiananmen massacre unfolded. That summer, 1 million Hong Kong people marched in protest. A second rush of emigrations followed, causing a 'brain drain' as Hong Kong's talented professionals decamped for Australia, Canada, the US and other countries that would grant them residency or citizenship. Hong Kongers of Chinese descent were not eligible for full British citizenship.

After years of difficult negotiations, the Basic Law was ratified by the National People's Congress in 1990. A mini-constitution for Hong Kong was provided in the Joint Declaration, guaranteeing a 'high degree of autonomy' on all matters except defence and foreign affairs for the next 50 years following the handover. Despite assurances, it sparked more fear in the financial community, and some foreign companies chose to move their operations to Singapore. Although democratic reform had not been encouraged during the colonial era, the British made efforts to safeguard

THIS PAGE (FROM LEFT): The last governor Chris Patten; the Legislative Council of Hong Kong is housed in the Old Supreme Court building.

OPPOSITE: Deng Xiaoping recognised that Hong Kong's economy could not assimilate into China's economic system overnight.

Hong Kong and restore confidence by introducing the Bill of Rights Ordinance 1991. Hong Kong's last governor Chris Patten tried to implement a democratic infrastructure, but most of his ideas did not meet China's approval. For example, he proposed to turn the legislature, previously made up of British appointees, into a fully elected body. Today, half of the legislative council is selected through direct elections.

hand it over

The handover took place in Hong Kong on June 30, 1997 with much pomp and circumstance; the kind of celebration that marks the end of an era. Held at the new wing of the Hong Kong Convention and Exhibition Centre in Wan Chai, the milestone event was attended by principal British guest Prince Charles; the Prime

Minister of the United Kingdom, Tony Blair; Chris Patten; Chairman of the People's Republic of China, Jiang Zemin; and Tung Chee-hwa, the first Chief Executive of the Hong Kong SAR. Tung Chee-hwa, a member of a prominent shipping family, had been favoured by China and elected by an 800-member election committee. He took office on July 1, 1997, a day after handover.

crisis management

The beginning of this new chapter presented a series of difficulties that would test Hong Kong's ability to bounce back. In 1998, the same year Hong Kong's spectacular new airport designed by Sir Norman Foster was opened on Lantau island, the Asian financial crisis struck.

Hong Kong suffered, but was not as hard hit as other countries in Asia such as Indonesia and even Singapore. Just three years later, China's entry into the World Trade Organisation (WTO) threatened to reinstate Shanghai as a rival. And in 2001, the September 11 bombings caused a global economic slowdown, causing Hong Kong's tourism sector to suffer greatly.

In the spring of 2003, the SARS virus broke out in Guangdong province and spread to Hong Kong. The city recoiled in fear as the government encouraged the use of medical masks and advised its residents to avoid crowded public places. The World Health Organisation (WHO) issued a travel warning that further ravaged Hong Kong's tourism industry, bringing visitor levels down to a 12-year low.

who's the chief

The resilient community survived; and approximately half a million took to the streets on July 1, 2003, SAR Establishment Day, to protest the anti-subversion Article 23 of the Basic Law. It proved an outlet for another issue on the minds of Hong Kong people, as a large number of protesters held up banners that

THIS PAGE: Hong Kongers protesting the anti-subversion Article 23 of the Basic Law.

OPPOSITE (FROM TOP): Fireworks lit up the sky to mark the handover; the bright red SAR flag flapping in the wind.

denounced Tung Chee-hwa for being 'too agreeable' to Beijing. Pro-democracy rallies have continued to draw thousands every July 1. Citing 'health concerns', Tung resigned in the middle of his second five-year term. In June 2005, former Chief Secretary Donald Tsang was elected to complete the remaining two years of Tung's term.

Tsang, famous for wearing bow ties, is recognised for bringing Hong Kong out of the Asian financial crisis in his previous role as Financial Secretary (1995–2001). When his proposals for democratic reforms were rejected for not going far enough in late 2005, Tsang announced that he would re-focus his efforts on the economy. Although his plans for a new government headquarters are controversial, Tsang is generally popular.

leader of the pack

Hong Kong has once again risen from the ashes. In 2003, Hong Kong and Beijing deepened their already extensive economic ties by signing the Closer Economic Partnership Arrangement (CEPA), giving Hong Kong trade advantages over foreign countries dealing with China.

The beleaguered tourism sector has been given a boost by increased Mainland-visitor numbers as China eases its travel restrictions. In addition to concerted efforts by the Hong Kong Tourism Board, major new attractions have drawn tourists from around the region. One example is Hong Kong Disneyland, a joint development between the Hong Kong government and Disney which opened in September 2005, and which is especially popular with the Mainland Chinese.

Aside from a flourishing tourist industry, there has been a marked rise in exports. Unemployment rates are at their lowest levels in years. Consumer confidence has returned and the avid Hong Kong shoppers are back. Although Shanghai and the special economic zone of Shenzhen are hot on its heels, Hong Kong is still leading the pack.

THIS PAGE (FROM TOP): Mickey Mouse is a new beacon for tourism, especially from China; Disney magic now takes up a part of Lantau.

OPPOSITE: Fast forward: the future seems bright for this city in constant motion.

...Hong Kong is still leading the pack.

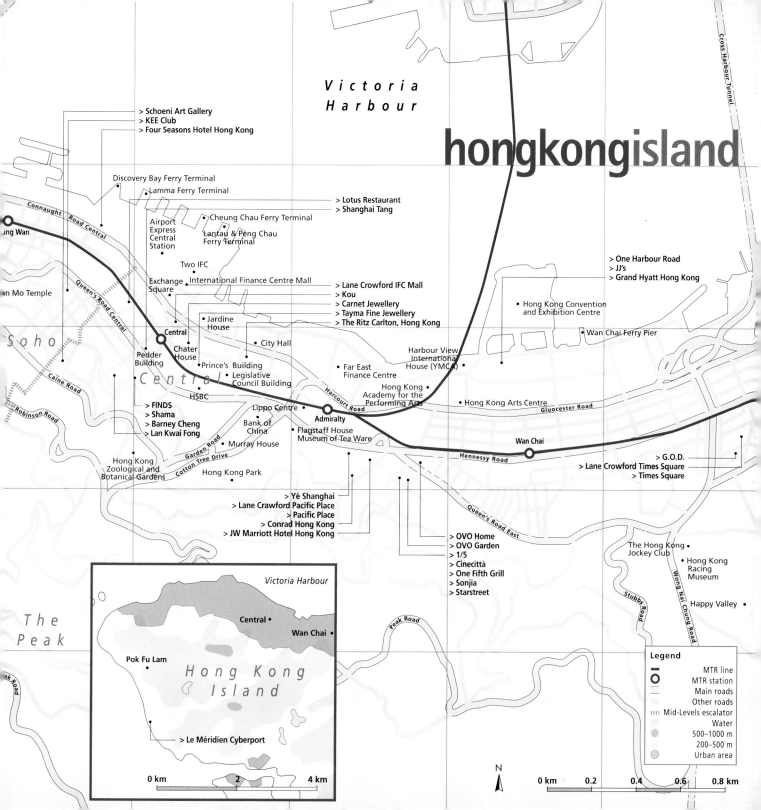

hongkongisland

Victoria Harbour

> Schoeni Art Gallery
> KEE Club
> Four Seasons Hotel Hong Kong

Discovery Bay Ferry Terminal
Lamma Ferry Terminal

> Lotus Restaurant
> Shanghai Tang

Cheung Chau Ferry Terminal

Airport
Express
Central
Station

Lantau & Peng Chau
Ferry Terminal

Connaught Road Central

ung Wan

Two IFC

> One Harbour Road
> JJ's
> Grand Hyatt Hong Kong

Exchange
Square

International Finance Centre Mall

> Lane Crowford IFC Mall
> Kou
> Carnet Jewellery
> Tayma Fine Jewellery
> The Ritz Carlton, Hong Kong

Hong Kong Convention
and Exhibition Centre

an Mo Temple

Queen's Road Central

Jardine
House

Wan Chai Ferry Pier

Soho

Central

Pedder
Building

Chater
House

City Hall

Prince's Building

Harbour View
International
House (YMCA)

Central

Legislative
Council Building

Far East
Finance Centre

Caine Road

HSBC

Hong Kong
Academy for the
Performing Arts

Hong Kong Arts Centre

Robinson Road

> FINDS
> Shama
> Barney Cheng
> Lan Kwai Fong

Lippo Centre

Admiralty

Harcourt Road

Gluocester Road

Bank of
China

Flagstaff House
Museum of Tea Ware

Wan Chai

Garden Road

Murray House

Hennessy Road

> G.O.D.

> Lane Crowford Times Square
> Times Square

Cotton Tree Drive

Hong Kong
Zoological and
Botanical Gardens

Hong Kong Park

Queen's Road East

> Yè Shanghai
> Lane Crawford Pacific Place
> Pacific Place
> Conrad Hong Kong
> JW Marriott Hotel Hong Kong

The Hong Kong
Jockey Club

Hong Kong
Racing
Museum

> OVO Home
> OVO Garden
> 1/5
> Cinecittà
> One Fifth Grill
> Sonjia
> Starstreet

Stubbs Road

Wong Nai Chung Road

Happy Valley

*The
Peak*

Victoria Harbour

Central •
Wan Chai •

Peak Road

Pok Fu Lam •

*Hong Kong
Island*

ak Road

> Le Méridien Cyberport

0 km   2   4 km

N

Legend

○ MTR line
○ MTR station
— Main roads
— Other roads
┊┊┊ Mid-Levels escalator
Water
500–1000 m
200–500 m
Urban area

0 km   0.2   0.4   0.6   0.8 km

buy me, love

If shopping were an Olympic sport, Hong Kong would have multiple gold medals. It's practised as an activity rather than a necessity, particularly on weekends with the whole family. To suit long office hours, some areas stay open until 10 pm or later. Whether shoppers have a specific product in mind is irrelevant for a population that loves all things branded.

In terms of purchasing power per capita, Hong Kong has one of the highest in Asia and it shows. From the shipping magnate in a custom-made suit to the Hakka hat wearing street-sweeper, everyone seems to be carrying the latest mobile phone. There are arguably more luxury cars on the roads of Hong Kong than in any other cosmopolitan capital (you might not have a home big enough to entertain, but you'll drive to the restaurant in style). The trussed up tai-tais (literally 'Mrs', a term for wealthy ladies) are walking advertisements for designer goods, from the sparkling jewels in their ears, to their haute couture outfits, down to their branded heels. Even secretaries save up to buy the latest Louis Vuitton or Gucci handbag.

making a sale

Shopping in Hong Kong is not what it used to be. It's better. Despite some of the highest retail rents in the world, product prices remain competitive. It helps that there is no sales tax, although one is being considered. Shopping is also the top activity of tourists, many of whom visit Hong Kong expressly for that purpose. More international brands are available now than ever before. Their elegant boutiques are conveniently housed in spectacular new malls designed by renowned architects, providing air-conditioned comfort for anyone and everyone away from the humid, hurried streets.

PAGE 30: City lights: the streets pulsate with life at night.

THIS PAGE (FROM TOP): Merchandise arranged for maximum tantalisation captures the yearning of passers-by; shoes in every conceivable shade will satisfy even the fussiest shopper.

OPPOSITE: You cannot go far in Hong Kong without coming across a sale.

Nostalgic bargain-hunters lament the retail upgrade, but the discounts are still there if you know where to look. There are biannual sales (January to February, and July to August) that slash prices by 50 to 90 per cent, and retailers host warehouse sales to clear stock—some even have outlet stores. Jewellery is still a wonderful buy, thanks to the absence of tax or duty, and a growing number of Hong Kong-based designers such as Tayma Fine Jewellery, Carnet Jewellery and Covatta Design make exciting, one-of-a-kind pieces. The tailors, famous for dressing visiting celebrities in less than 24 hours, are still turning tourists into tuxedo-clad James Bond look-alikes and crafting custom-made shirts and suits to boot.

Even fine Chinese antiques can be better priced in Hong Kong than in China. For cheap and cheerful finds, there are always the colourful street markets. Between the prohibitively expensive and throwaway prices, one hole in the market used to be mid-priced items, a void which is now steadily being filled by local and Mainland China brands, as well as the arrival of 'high street' labels from Europe and the US. Young local brands do struggle. However, even they have opportunities to put their wares on the market; through avenues such as lively little commercial buildings in Causeway Bay and Tsim Sha Tsui, fairs, the Internet and up-and-coming areas like Soho (before rents skyrocket). In fact, there are few things you cannot buy in Hong Kong these days.

china doll

Western modes of dress became the dominant choice long ago, and in recent times Chinese tailoring has been reserved for weddings and certain formal events, especially in the case of women.

A few renowned specialist tailors and staid Chinese department stores have survived the economic rollercoaster through the years, but neither helped change the perception that cheongsams and the like were old-fashioned or, worse, touristy. Then China became a source of inspiration in the 1990s. Nouveau cheongsams were strutted down the Paris catwalks. Major auction houses noticed a renewed interest in

THIS PAGE (FROM TOP): Shrines to style innovatively display the latest fashions; Shanghai Tang's beautifully appointed stores recall a glamorous era.
OPPOSITE (FROM TOP): Sumptuous spas make it easy to escape from the city; Harbour City is a shopping haven made up of four connected malls.

Chinese antiquities. And films like Wong Kar-wai's *In the Mood for Love* became international arthouse hits. Enter the new Chinese brands like Shanghai Tang, who have put a modern, fashionable spin on traditional clothing and lifestyle products. It took Hong Kong a few years to be seduced; but the Mainland is catching on quickly.

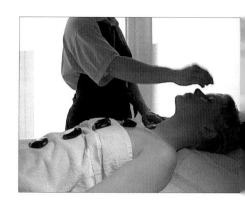

spa the difference

Spas in Hong Kong run the gamut, from some of the most pampering treatments in the world to amazingly affordable massages in basic but acceptable surroundings. A new fascination with slimming and beauty treatments promising miraculous results has unfortunately spawned a few unscrupulous peddlers, but these are monitored by Hong Kong's vigilant Consumer Council. At the top end, Hong Kong spas represent a hybrid of East and West, merging the best possible treatments, approaches to service and sumptuous interiors to provide the ultimate 'spa journey,' as they like to call it. Many of the most highly-rated are tucked away inside five-star hotels. At the Grand Hyatt Hong Kong an entire floor is dedicated to Plateau, a spa with ingeniously designed overnight rooms where guests can enjoy in-room treatments then continue to relax when they're done.

northern exposure

Tsim Sha Tsui across the harbour in Kowloon is either a paradise or an assault on the senses, depending on the shopper. Hovering around MTR (Mass Transit Railway) exits, the Star Ferry and Nathan Road, pamphlet-carrying hopefuls accost people with offers of tailoring services, pashminas and imitation watches. One could spend days in Harbour City, a complex of four connected malls with hundreds of designer stores, several hotels and a cruise ship terminal. A highlight of the area is the legendary Peninsula hotel, with its rich history

inextricably linked to that of Hong Kong. Afternoon tea in The Lobby or a drink in the Philippe Starck-designed Felix restaurant provides a decadent break from shopping. Major thoroughfare Nathan Road boasts shops of all kinds; it is most often associated with electronics and camera shops, though not always reputable ones. Nearby Granville Road, once a haven for factory outlets, is a popular source of local brands and bargains. Insiders know to duck into the Granville Circuit alley and enter Rise Commercial Building—three floors of tiny shops displaying the works of young designers, cool Japanese trinkets and random trend items.

Wherever you go, there is sure to be a mall nearby. They are spread along major MTR stops from Tsim Sha Tsui, to the new Langham Place in Mong Kok, across to Festival Walk in Kowloon Tong; so large it also holds a mega-cinema complex and Hong Kong's largest ice rink. Kowloon is also home to the most interesting street markets and is the best place for adventurous shoppers and culture vultures alike.

above and beyond

Across the harbour on Hong Kong Island, Central business district is less chaotic, easier to navigate and more Westernised—which spells boring to some. Here, elegant malls—Prince's Building, Alexandra House, The Landmark, Chater House and ifc mall, to name a few—are filled with luxury boutiques. They are connected by overpasses so that one need not descend to street level; a blessing in the hotter months. It is, however, worth crossing the road to the gargoyle-topped Pedder Building, constructed in 1924.

On the ground floor is the fabulously decorated boutique of Shanghai Tang, an upscale purveyor of modern Chinese lifestyle products; upper floors house designer label discount and consignment stores, a children's one-stop shop, kitchen supplies stores, and the delightful China Tee Club. Down the road, even this affluent area offers the market experience in parallel Li Yuen Street East and Li Yuen Street West, better known as 'The Lanes', where they sell everything from cheap plastic watches and toys to well-made leather handbags.

Wherever you go, there is sure to be a mall nearby.

THIS PAGE (FROM TOP): Central's major buildings are conveniently connected by overhead walkways; shopping and dining go late into the night.

OPPOSITE (FROM LEFT): Discounts on jade at Yau Ma Tei; Temple Street Market comes alive at night.

precious cargo

The famous Central-Mid-Levels escalator stops off at two shopping hotspots, Hollywood Road and Soho. Known as the main strip for antique furniture, maps, ceramics, jade, rugs, textiles and contemporary Asian art, Hollywood Road is home to wonderfully knowledgeable experts and a few charlatans to keep would-be collectors on their toes. Disappointment can be averted, though, by buying only from reputable dealers, requesting certificates of authenticity, and not believing bargains that seem too good to be true. It is important to note that China does not allow pieces over 120 years old to leave the country. Incredibly, prices for Chinese antiques are often better in Hong Kong than on the Mainland, where interest from the new wealthy class has bumped up market prices. A few highly respected dealers have chosen not to be associated with the area, taking up residence in Prince's Building, for example, and more unique spots like one of the few preserved houses in Central set against the backdrop of skyscrapers.

As its name might suggest, Soho is an eclectic mix of shops, galleries and restaurants. The charming neighbourhood's potential was first noted even before the escalator began bringing a constant flow of people up the previously terraced streets in 1994. These days, shoppers go there to visit fashion designers' ateliers, contemporary art galleries, vintage stores, and the few remaining shops selling everyday chinaware such as cheap blue-and-white fish bowls.

east side story

Moving east along the tram tracks, Admiralty is essentially a series of buildings that bridge Central and Wan Chai; comprising shopping malls, hotels and office blocks. Pacific Place mall is yet another example of the city's wealth, with its elegant atmosphere and high-end tenants. Overhead walkways connect it to less glamorous edifices—Queensway Plaza, United Centre and Admiralty Centre—which feature more affordable shopping, tailors and some of Hong Kong's best custom shoemakers.

More intrepid shoppers enjoy a stroll through the once-mean streets of Suzie Wong in Wan Chai. Thrifty residents have their curtains and upholstery made on Queen's Road East, where hilarious parodies of brand names such as 'Giormani' are de rigeur. They buy fresh produce at the wet market, and continue along Tai Yuen Street for cheap tsotskes and Thai grocery stores that sometimes serve authentic food. Parallel streets also offer 'factory outlets' filled with generic brand T-shirts and casual wear at low prices. Technophiles go mad for the reasonably priced offerings (both genuine and counterfeit) at the Wan Chai Computer Centre. Lockhart Road, the source of bathroom fixtures, industrial carpets and tiles for contractors and home builders, stretches from Wan Chai to Causeway Bay.

While many Westerners tend to stay within the confines of Central, Causeway Bay is where the locals love to shop and eat on the island. There are Japanese department stores, big malls such as Times Square with its great glass elevator on the exterior, and little rabbit warrens of local designers found in youth-oriented malls such as Island Beverly. Near Victoria Park, Hong Kong's version of Central Park, Windsor House is an odd mix of supermarket, department store, cinema, toyshops and entire floors of legitimate computer products. In the narrow maze of Causeway Bay's streets, new-generation designers, surfing gear suppliers, markets like Jardine's Bazaar, and quirky dining concepts (for instance, there's a café that has cats wandering around and invites cat owners to bring their pets along) make for wonderful little discoveries.

to market, to market

Almost every area has a street market that warrants a visit as much for the cheap finds as for the sheer spectacle. In Kowloon, Temple Street Night Market in Jordan is open in the afternoon but is at its best at night, alive with lit-up street stalls, fortune-tellers and occasional

Cantonese opera performances. In Yau Ma Tei, the Jade Market overflows with beautiful jade, plastic, and semi-precious trinkets that invariably look more impressive away from the dusty stalls stocked with hundreds of other similar items. Stanley Market on the south side of Hong Kong Island exemplifies the city's shift from back-of-the-truck discounted labels to legitimate goods. Although Stanley Market is still filled with cheap clothing and souvenirs, shoppers now go for kids clothes, affordable brand name luggage, and wonderfully priced linens.

curtain call

Where there used to be a dearth of cultural events, Hong Kong now boasts a comprehensive calendar of performances, exhibitions and festivals featuring international and local talent from the worlds of music, dance, theatre, film, and fine art. Plans are underway to develop a 40-hectare (99-acre) integrated arts, cultural and entertainment district in West Kowloon, although aggressive land reclamation for such projects and the notion that creativity should be centralised have both caused some controversy. The arts in Hong Kong are underrated, even if they are admittedly not yet up to the standards of London or New York. One glance at the local newspaper listings proves that creativity is actually on the rise.

by invitation

Several festivals have made great strides in raising the profile of the arts in a city more concerned with the bottom line. The Hong Kong Arts Festival has presented exceptional international performances and exhibitions since its first inception in 1973 and; in the process, it has cultivated public appreciation, paving the way for homegrown talent. The festival relies partly on funding from the government's Leisure and Cultural Services Department and the Hong Kong Jockey Club Charities Trust; two organisations that provide grants for numerous creative endeavours. Staged annually over three to four weeks, performance-starved residents would rush back and forth across the harbour—

THIS PAGE (FROM TOP): A growing performing arts scene now attracts full houses; Arts hub, the Fringe Club.
OPPOSITE: A rainbow of lights highlight the curvilinear Cultural Centre.

...Hong Kong now boasts a comprehensive calendar of performances, exhibitions...

THIS PAGE (FROM TOP): *The Rockit Hong Kong Music Festival keeps rock and roll music alive; Princess Superstar at Rockit.*

OPPOSITE (FROM TOP):
Swirling lanterns at the 2005 Biennale Hong Kong Response Exhibition at the Hong Kong Museum of Art; geometrical lines and shapes of the atrium at the Hong Kong Art Centre.

from City Hall to the Cultural Centre, and perhaps even farther afield to venues such as Sha Tin Town Hall in the New Territories—trying to get their year's fill of culture within a dizzying time frame. Today, the festival is still about a manic period of rushing from venue to venue, but there is now the promise of more outings during the rest of the year.

The Fringe Club has also been instrumental in creating an environment for artists to create and show their work through, as its name suggests, a slightly more adventurous approach to promoting the arts. It has hosted an annual arts series since 1983, now known as the City Fringe Festival. Its colonial-style headquarters in Central, built in 1913, is a community gathering place and has multiple gallery spaces, theatres, a rehearsal room, a pottery studio and showroom, a roof garden, and bar-cafés.

rock it

As of 2003, Hong Kong's growing live music scene even has an outdoor rock festival. The Rockit Hong Kong Music Festival is a phenomenal three-day weekend of rock and dance music in Causeway Bay's Victoria Park. Artists and DJs from around the globe play on several stages while a mix of students, financiers and Lamma hippies cut loose or sit on the grass and soak up the atmosphere.

A more recent highlight is the Man Hong Kong International Literary Festival, which was launched in 2001 as a little weekend event and has grown to become the most respected English-language literary festival in Asia. In 2006, 60 authors were in Hong Kong for the 10-day programme, including Nobel Prize laureate Seamus Heaney, whose lecture sold out to an audience of 700.

trip of the eye

Crowds descend on the world of fine art for Hong Kong Art Walk, a fun charity event and the art appreciator's version of a pub-crawl. Ticket-holders have open access to over 40 galleries where food and drinks, supplied by participating restaurants, are laid out. The trail of exhibitions leads from Wan Chai to Central, Soho and Sheung Wan (and, by shuttle bus, Aberdeen), creating a friendly atmosphere in which to view art. The lively evening ambience is especially helpful for those who might have the means but not the courage to venture into austere galleries alone.

Hong Kong has over 20 museums, 12 of which are managed by the Leisure and Cultural Services Department. The short list includes: Hong Kong Museum of Art, Hong Kong Space Museum, University Museum and Art Gallery, Flagstaff House Museum of Tea Ware, Hong Kong Museum of Coastal Defence, Hong Kong Museum of History, Hong Kong Museum of Medical Sciences, and the Hong Kong Science Museum.

for art's sake

Events like the Art Walk, special exhibitions, and record-breaking sales at top auction houses all showcase Hong Kong as a centre for highly collectible contemporary Asian art from Hong Kong, China, Vietnam, Indonesia, the Philippines, Thailand, Korea, and beyond. In 2000, Hong Kong-raised art historian Claire Hsu founded the Asia Art Archive (AAA) in collaboration with renowned art expert Chang Tsong-zung and Hong Kong Jockey Club Chairman Ronald Arculli. The pioneering non-profit research centre was started in response to the incredible number of contemporary Asian art exhibitions that

were sprouting up worldwide at the time. The AAA has since grown too large for its original space, but continues to acquire and catalogue all related materials in an effort to support and promote the wider understanding of contemporary Asian art. Addressing the challenge placed on all young artists—finding a place to show and work in this high-rent city—Para/Site is one of Hong Kong's best independent art spaces. Conveniently located in Sheung Wan, its success is partly due to its proximity to Central and funding from the Hong Kong Arts Development Council. Due to open in 2007, the Hong Kong Jockey Club's creative arts centre is a 9,290-sq m (100,000-sq ft) space in Shek Kip Mei that aims to be a self-supporting cultural hub where artists can rent a space and enjoy the support of all the necessary facilities to practise and display their art.

market for creativity

Attitudes towards the arts have begun to change and, although parents would still prefer to see their children become doctors and lawyers, there is a growing acceptance of art as a career. Several factors have made it easier to survive in one of the most expensive cities in the world. There is more support for young artists from governmental and private institutions. Hong Kong artists from various fields have been recognised on the international stage. Disneyland, opened in 2005, has created many new opportunities for performers. To put it in business-minded terms, there is a market for artists. The dilemma now is how to foster creativity. The government has acknowledged that Hong Kong lags behind other 'world-class' cities because of its lack of creativity and related industries. Students may score high marks in mathematics when compared with other countries, but the exam-driven education system does not seem to have time for nurturing artistic creativity.

One beacon is the Hong Kong Academy for Performing Arts (APA), founded by the government in 1984. Although Hong Kong's universities do offer arts degree programmes, the APA is the city's

THIS PAGE (FROM LEFT):
Choreographer and dancer Youya Shinjo performs the dance 'Chaser' at the Hong Kong Dance Festival 2006; leading funnyman Stephen Chow gets his own spot on the Avenue of Stars.

OPPOSITE (FROM TOP):
The legendary Shaw Studio, responsible for a great deal of Hong Kong film's catalogue; Hong Kong lead actor Tony Leung goes for another take.

only tertiary institution of its kind, nurturing talent in six schools: dance, drama, film and television, music, technical arts and Chinese traditional theatre. The vast APA building, sitting on the Wan Chai waterfront, has training and research facilities, as well as a number of performance venues used for student performances that are open to the public, and professional shows. In an effort to bring the arts to the wider community, they encourage students to participate in outreach activities.

reel deal

Film, a celebrated Hong Kong medium, has been an artform easier to sell. In addition to almost 60 cinemas with 200 screens showing mostly Chinese- and English-language movies, the city hosts The Hong Kong International Film Festival every year. It shows more than 200 films and several retrospective or thematic programmes over 16 days. Cultural institutes and consulates of various countries are also active in Hong Kong. Every autumn, the MAX! German language film festival screens works from Austria, Switzerland and Germany; Le French May presents a month-long programme comprising opera, dance, music, theatre, cinema and fine art from France. The Hong Kong Film Archive, another Leisure and Cultural Services Department initiative, works to collect and preserve prints and artefacts. In order to promote Hong Kong film, it develops exhibitions and publications and provides public research facilities.

Hong Kong film is famous for its martial arts and distinctive choreography. Abroad, its visionaries—think Bruce Lee, Jackie Chan, John Woo—have had a cult following for years. At home, they are gods. No discussion of Hong Kong cinema would be complete without a mention of the Shaw Brothers, the most influential and enduring forces in the industry. Sir Run Run Shaw, the youngest brother born in 1907, has been a colourful character in Hong Kong society for decades. Although Hong Kong film made its name with martial arts, it was built on Cantonese opera movies, popular from its humble beginnings in the late 1890s well into the 1970s. The 1980s and early 1990s were boom years that saw Hong Kong rise to become the third largest motion

picture industry in the world, after Bollywood and Hollywood. Another vehicle for the promotion of Hong Kong pop culture are its extremely popular romantic comedies, which star a rotating cast of pretty, young starlets. Hong Kong's importance to world cinema has been highlighted by the release of Hollywood blockbusters such as *The Matrix* which borrowed heavily from elements in its cinematic history. Quentin Tarantino, a diehard fan, has taken it further. Some even claim movies like *Kill Bill* and *Reservoir Dogs* are copied directly from *City of Fire* (Ringo Lam). Whatever the case, they have brought the city's movie industry to a wider global audience, and aided the international success of other works including Ang Lee's *Crouching Tiger, Hidden Dragon* and Wong Kar-wai's *In the Mood for Love*.

troupe stories

Larger venues such as the Cultural Centre on the Tsim Sha Tsui waterfront run audience-building programmes including lunchtime concerts; and many performance halls offer subtitles in English, Chinese, or both. For over 30 years, the Hong Kong Philharmonic Orchestra has enriched the community with a diverse repertoire, from opera-in-concert performances and the symphonic classics to music that sits outside the traditional orchestra scope, including Canto-Pop. Led by distinguished Artistic Director and Chief Conductor Edo de Waart, its remarkable ensemble of Chinese and international artists gives over 100 concerts a year. Guest performers have included such legends as Isaac Stern and Yo-Yo Ma, Chinese artists Lang Lang and Yundi Li, and Hong Kong pop stars like Jacky Cheung and Sandy Lam. The heritage of Chinese traditional music is preserved by the Hong Kong Chinese Orchestra, which focuses exclusively on Chinese works arranged for each concert and played on bowed strings, wind, plucked instruments and percussion.

Cantonese opera, with its intricate folklore, symbolic movements and demanding singing techniques, is performed at Temple Street Night Market almost every night (predominantly by amateurs), and in concerts put on by the 10 professional troupes

THIS PAGE: Bruce Lee continues to have a strong presence in contemporary culture.

OPPOSITE (FROM LEFT): Makeup is a crucial component of Cantonese opera, painstakingly applied, in the same way it was a hundred years ago; symbolic makeup and costumes identify each opera's character.

based in Hong Kong Island. Similarly, dozens of amateur and professional theatre groups stage plays in Cantonese or English around town. They include the Hong Kong Repertory Theatre, Ming Ri Theatre Company for professional child actors, and the avant-garde Zuni Icosahedron.

The Chung Ying Theatre Company, whose name is composed of the Cantonese words for Chinese and English, is known for original productions by local playwrights, and presents works by foreign directors through its close connections with theatre companies abroad. The Hong Kong Ballet is Hong Kong's first professional ballet company and trains dancers in its vocational school, while others like the modern City Contemporary Dance Company and Hong Kong Dance Company have brought other schools of dance to the scene.

THIS PAGE (FROM TOP): Every detail is considered at KEE Club; lunch time at Chee Kee—it serves traditional Cantonese style wanton noodles.

OPPOSITE (FROM TOP): Meticulously prepared cuisine at FINDS; discreet, stylish and comfortable—KEE is all a private club should be.

have you eaten?

Walk into a Hong Kong office at 1.01 pm, and all you're likely to find is an eerie emptiness. Alien abduction? No, it's lunchtime. The moneymaking frenzy has been temporarily transferred to countless restaurants around this fast-paced city; a ritual observed daily between 1—2 pm.

So great is the emphasis on food, the greeting "Nei sik jor fan mei?" ("Have you eaten?") is often used as a substitute for hello, or "Nei hou ma?" ("How are you?"). Dining out is extremely popular and, because the majority of homes are too small for entertaining, social and family gatherings are often held in restaurants. It is not uncommon, for example, to witness a wedding banquet at nearby tables.

Hong Kong's vast selection of restaurants caters to a culture passionate about eating. The major dining areas are Causeway Bay, Lan Kwai Fong, Soho, Stanley, Tsim Sha Tsui, Sai Kung and Lamma, but signs on almost every street advertise food from most regions on earth. They include various cuisines—Chinese, Japanese, Thai, Vietnamese, Indian, Nepalese, Indonesian, Egyptian, Lebanese, American, Argentinean, Mexican, Moroccan, Italian, French, Spanish, Australian, German, Russian, and even Scandinavian. For example, current hotspot FINDS (an acronym for Finland, Iceland, Norway, Denmark and Sweden) has transferred Hong Kong's fascination with Scandinavian design to its food and drink. The variety also extends to the price range; from the disappearing, cheap dai paidong street stalls to lavish temples of haute cuisine and design created by award-winning international chefs.

members only

Exclusivity, appealing across the globe, is taken to new heights in Hong Kong. Private country and dining clubs have allowed affluent expatriates and residents to escape from the crowded streets since Hong Kong first became a colony. Many of the original clubs such as the Hong Kong Club are still in operation, though in modern and more racially inclusive forms. The concept began to morph into a new phenomenon called private dining or private kitchens in the late 1990s.

In contrast to restaurant chains, private kitchens such as Xi Yan are labours of love, often started by ex-lawyers or business professionals who would like to indulge their passion for food. Like speakeasies, they are rarely visible from the street and can only be found by word-of-mouth. They have fixed-price set menus targeted at the true foodie;

and are devised to accommodate often tiny kitchen spaces while highlighting the chef's genius. Because alcohol licenses are so hard to come by, many allow diners to bring their own wines without charging corkage—a welcome bonus since the import tax on alcohol makes ordering a bottle of wine exorbitant. Reservations need to be made months in advance and seating is usually very limited. So, of course, everyone wants to go. A few years on, the underground movement has risen above street level. It has also been replicated in cities from Singapore to San Francisco, and certain chefs have even become celebrities with their own TV shows.

home cooking

Despite an eager appetite for new taste experiences, Hong Kong thankfully still specialises in traditional Cantonese cuisine. Intricate and sophisticated in style; it is subtle in taste in comparison with the spiciness of Szechuan, the sweetness of Shanghainese, or the stodginess of Beijing's dumplings, noodles and meats—all of which are also devoured with delight in Hong Kong. Fresh ingredients, particularly seafood and vegetables, are cooked quickly at high temperatures to seal in the flavours. Cantonese specialties span the controversial shark's fin soup, char siu (marinated, barbecued pork shoulder), pigeon, abalone and bird's nest soup; but dim sum is by far the most popular delicacy.

touching the heart

Dim sum is a Hong Kong institution. It is enjoyed during yum cha (tea drinking), which is the social act of enjoying not only Chinese tea, but also food and conversation. The dim sum menu features exquisite little dumplings, buns and pastries, usually presented in servings of three or four pieces in bamboo steam baskets for breakfast (7.30—10 am) or lunch (11.30 am—2.30 pm). Strictly a daytime treat, attempts to order dim sum any later in the day would be like requesting a cappuccino after dinner in Rome—it's simply not done.

Some restaurants still serve dim sum the old, theatrical way. For example, at Maxim's Palace in City Hall or the nearby Victoria Seafood Restaurant, waitresses push carts filled with specific items between the tables, shouting out names of dishes. Once flagged down (the shy will go hungry), the waitress stamps her unique chop on a card that is kept on your table and tallied for the bill at the end of the meal. More modern venues such as yè shanghai serve new and original interpretations of dim sum via a more serene à la carte system to match their sophisticated interior design. There are said to be over 2,000 varieties of dim sum with creative chefs crafting new inventions all the time, so choosing from the wide selection can be daunting. Amongst the most popular are: har gau (steamed shrimp encased dumplings in translucent wraps), siu mai (steamed pork dumplings), cheung fan (steamed rice flour rolls flavoured with spring onions, shrimp, pork, or beef), and char siu bao (light, steamed buns stuffed with barbecued pork), not to mention char siu so (barbecued pork in a flaky pastry). As your list of favourites grows, the true difficulty is not in ordering but in learning when to stop.

in the neighbourhood

The local food experience does not, however, begin and end with dim sum. The neighbourhood teahouse or cha chan teng is a hub of activity rarely witnessed by foreigners, but it is so much a part of Hong Kong life that it has been featured in countless movies and locally-produced TV shows. The interior is usually quite basic, with folding tables and chairs, and a cash register at the door to pay as you leave.

Often run by families who work long hours and need to take their meals quickly, a table is sometimes cleared for two to three generations of relatives to have their own meal together amongst their clientele. One is expected to share the table with other customers, and non-smoking sections do not exist. The formula is replicated by restaurant chain Tsui Wah. Their 'Hong Kong-style Western' menus are an odd reminder of Hong Kong's colonial past with yuen yueng (an unexpected mix of coffee, introduced by the British, and black Chinese tea), the potent yit lai cha (strong black

THIS PAGE (FROM LEFT): *Noodles in dumpling soup, a classic staple; Yung Kee is famous for its roast goose, crisp and succulent.*

OPPOSITE (FROM TOP): *Fresh siew mai, a popular dim sum item, is served traditionally in its bamboo steamer; waitresses at the famous City Hall Maxim's Palace are kept busy during a hectic lunch.*

...restaurants offer fresh seafood...

tea with rich, sweet condensed milk), French toast served as a snack, sandwiches, and rice and pasta dishes with unusual twists. Looks can be deceiving. Some of the most authentic Hong Kong restaurants look unpromising at first glance, but serve delectable specialities such as wonton soup (noodle soup with shrimp dumplings), or congee (rice porridge) and yau char gwai (deep-fried dough strips). Street hawkers sell snacks of curried fish balls or squid on wooden skewers, sweet gai dan jai (literally 'little eggs', round treats made from coconut-flavoured batter poured into a special waffle iron heated over coals), and, in winter, roasted chestnuts and taro root.

Amidst the towering skyscrapers, it's easy to forget that Hong Kong is surrounded by water, with a number of fishing villages surprisingly close to the commercial hubs. In areas such as Sai Kung, Lei Yue Mun and Lamma island, al fresco restaurants offer fresh seafood and a casual, laid-back alternative to the urban jungle. Diners may choose from the catches of the day displayed in the restaurant's tanks but they can be quite expensive; whereas regular menu items are fresh too and more reasonably-priced.

sweet endings

Red beans, coconut milk, black sesames, ginger and sago might sound more like a concoction by an avant-garde restaurant like El Bulli in Spain, but these are just some of the key ingredients in delicious traditional Chinese desserts. Chinese restaurants usually offer a limited choice at the end of a meal, but dedicated Chinese dessert houses offer a cornucopia of surprising flavours. There are custard-like puddings, such as the popular mango pudding and steamed milk in two layers. Sweet soups vary from hot red bean to cold coconut, served with sweet dumplings, sago or fruit. Tong yuen, for example, is a heavenly combination of glutinous rice balls filled with black sesame paste and served hot in a sweet, spicy ginger broth. And there's the mouth-watering combination of diced mangos and sago in coconut milk. Fruits from around the region—mango, lychee, watermelon, honeydew—are so popular, the Hui Lau Shan dessert chain focuses solely on fruit-based desserts and fresh sliced fruit.

THIS PAGE (FROM TOP): Cheery-coloured chairs of a typical teahouse; egg tarts from the popular Tai Cheong Bakery.

OPPOSITE (FROM LEFT): Jumbo, the floating restaurant famous for its kitsch decorations, now with the chic Top Deck restaurant; fresh catch of the day.

Although not originally part of the southern China diet, bread and baked goods were also cannibalised so long ago they now exist in a their own category. Records show that in 1857, one disgruntled baker tried to rid Hong Kong of the British by adding arsenic to his bread, but misjudged the amount. None of his victims died, although many fell ill. Baked goods are generally reserved for breakfast, dessert or a snack, as rice and noodles still dominate during meals. Chinese bakeries sell signature items such as bo lo bau ('pineapple bread', sweet buns with caramelised tops that resemble pineapples but do not contain the fruit) and dan tart (baked custard egg tarts in a flaky pastry), also available in the typical dim sum selection.

When legendary egg tart shop, Tai Cheong Bakery, was forced to close because of rising rents, there was uproar. On its last day, customers lined up around the block outside the humble hole-in-the-wall—with the requisite photos of famous patrons on its walls—to get their last taste. In true Hong Kong style, the owners re-emerged across the road a few months later and the roaring trade is back.

THIS PAGE (FROM TOP): In party central, they've seen it all; Lan Kwai Fong is just steps away from the Central district.

OPPOSITE (FROM TOP): Aqua Spirit's commanding views; shaken or stirred, drink it up in Hong Kong.

all night long

Hong Kong's nightlife is dangerous. The threat comes not from thugs in this reassuringly safe city, but from the never-ending partying. Hong Kong's seemingly tireless residents know how to work hard and play harder. After office hours, many prefer to go out before heading home. Shops and markets stay open until 10 pm in certain areas. Movie theatres sell out to full houses. A growing number are attending performances and cultural events. Foot reflexology houses welcome weary customers late into the night. And every evening of the week, trendy bars, thumping nightclubs and neighbourhood pubs are packed with thrill-seekers.

Most of the action takes place in Central, but there is also plenty of entertainment in Wan Chai, Causeway Bay, and Tsim Sha Tsui. Just up the hill from Central's financial and business centre, Lan Kwai Fong is a circuit of over 100 restaurants, bars and nightclubs. Although popular for lunch, it really comes alive at night when people

from all walks of life converge on the former hawkers bazaar to let off some steam. Couples meet for pre-dinner cocktails, bankers celebrate billion-dollar deals, friends catch up, and singletons go on the hunt. On weekends and holidays, the party spills out into the street and is a sight to behold.

In the surrounding area, a host of satellite venues offer chic and sometimes mellower options. The social set, models, business moguls and visiting celebrities congregate in exclusive upstairs clubs, such as KEE Club. A few streets up, the charming Soho turns the buzzing energy down a notch amidst a cosy burrow of restaurants, bistros, wine bars, and lounges that attract a quieter crowd. To the east of Lan Kwai Fong, Wan Chai has undergone a revival from seedy red-light district to an alternative dining and drinking destination. That is not to say the girly bars have gone. Now, a stroll down the street will take you past the garish photos and signs outside hostess bars to pubs showing football match telecasts, and cool new bars.

The further away from Central, the less Westernised the experience. In places like Causeway Bay and Tsim Sha Tsui, for example, thousands play rock star or diva for the night in mega karaoke facilities where private, catered rooms avert the humiliation of crooning in a public bar.

Bars in the most exclusive hotels here are hip-and-happening with luxurious interiors, fabulous cocktails and impeccable service. For a less conspicuous venue, the speakeasy trend that is already successful in the dining world has spread to bars. Insatiable night owls have recently been entertained by this new crop of secret bars that are impossible to find and require an introduction.

now hear this

Live music is finally making its voice heard. Where there was only saccharine Canto-Pop, talented Filipino bands playing old standards and a tiny but remarkable jazz club, now there is a burgeoning music scene featuring other genres such as rock.

Every week, places such as the Fringe Club in Central and JJ's in Wan Chai promote and feature live music nights that showcase local talent. International DJs fly in for events in tiny clubs, on beaches or even in the ballrooms of fancy hotels. The demand for clubbing venues in the post-rave era remains high, and after the big nightclubs close there are now numerous late-night lock-ins dotted around town to keep you dancing until 6 am.

urbane planning

Hong Kong or Heung Hong means 'fragrant harbour'. There are several theories about the source of that fragrance—some believe it came from local incense production, for example. However, what currently emanates from the waters is more accurately described as fusty, which would not have made quite as charming a name. Today, the harbour is, thankfully, less well-known for its odour and more famous for the eye-catching buildings that flank it on Kowloon and Hong Kong Island.

THIS PAGE (FROM TOP):
A DJ spins his magic;
the party crowd dances the
night away.
OPPOSITE (FROM LEFT): Wan Chai,
once the domain of Suzie
Wong, now has trendy
nightclubs, five star hotels and
prestigious office buildings;
the city that never sleeps.

Many of the skyscrapers are award-winning examples of contemporary architecture, but expanding upwards has been more a necessity than an act of vanity. Of its 1,104 sq km (426 sq miles), Hong Kong has very little flat land—approximately 200 sq km (77 sq miles). As a result, commercial and residential rents are some of the highest in the world. The lack of space has led to high population density in concentrated patches.

reclaiming the past

For decades, Hong Kong has been a fierce competitor in the race to build the tallest structure, and it has had its fair share of record holders. It can seem like a new building goes up every day. Ever resourceful and adaptable, the city simply reclaims more land when it runs out. Two ifc, the building from which Angelina Jolie jumps in the movie *Tomb Raider 2*, is a prime example; it was built entirely on reclaimed land and sits several large city blocks away from the original harbourfront, now occupied by some of the most prominent developments in Central. Hong Kong's relationship with its surrounding waters has evolved from one of its being a fishing village to one of Hong Kong as a metropolis. Originally chosen by the British for its harbour, a strategic location from which to conduct trade, the SAR continues to prosper from the sea. Little has been allowed to stand in the way of progress. Even the iconic Star Ferry Pier in Central is being relocated to make way for, yes, more land reclamation.

monumental effort

Hong Kong has about 80 structures that have been declared monuments under the Antiquities and Monuments Ordinance. They include ancient structures, temples, traditional ancestral halls, and historic buildings representing Chinese and colonial heritage. These sites are protected from development and are respectfully restored when necessary. Some have been designated for 'adaptive re-use', which has been controversial among some conservation groups.

THIS PAGE: Temples are the last few low structures in a city of towering skyscrapers.
OPPOSITE (FROM TOP): Major buildings are connected by pedestrian overpasses; graphic windows of a building.

Still a place of great contrasts—East and West, old and new, dilapidated and shiny— the fascinating city presents modern marvels immediately next to old, low-rise buildings scattered throughout its 18 districts.

go west

Hong Kong Island may only measure about 80 sq km (31 sq miles), but it manages to showcase a surprisingly diverse range of buildings. The Western and Mid-Levels districts retain their old charm even as the contemporary spirit of Central edges ever closer.

The island's soaring skyline is occasionally interrupted by quaint structures such as Western Market. The pretty four-storey, Edwardian-style building with bandaged brickwork on its corner towers was completed in 1906, then converted into a shopping and food destination after the government moved the fresh food market to new facilities in 1991. From the ground floor up it is filled with odd layers of handicraft, souvenir and fabric shops. At the top, there is a Chinese restaurant that comes with a dance floor to cater to the new local fascination with Salsa and ballroom dancing. The surrounding area still offers traditional sundries such as ceremonial paper offerings, dried seafood, medicinal herbs, and bird's nests for soup.

If you didn't know it was there, you might never see the large former Pathological Institute hidden behind trees in the Mid-Levels district above Western and Central. The red brick building was constructed in 1905 for bacteriological studies and was renamed the Pathological Institute after World War II. Now, it has been converted to the Hong Kong Museum of Medical Sciences.

finding your centre

As Mid-Levels turns into Central, the Central Police Station compound takes up a large plot of land with various buildings constructed between 1864 to 1925. The station, along with the adjacent former Central Magistracy (1914) and Victoria Prison (1841), has been the recent battleground of heritage conservationists versus developers. Collectively, the buildings were declared monuments in 1995 and display examples of Victorian, Edwardian and other architectural styles. Proposed plans for the 'adaptive re-use' of the site as a tourist attraction incorporating restaurants, shops and a museum or art galleries have sparked debates. There were even suggestions that some of the buildings should be put up for tender.

THIS PAGE: Looking into Central from the Harbour, Hong Kong's eclectic architecture.

OPPOSITE (FROM TOP): Blindfolded Themis stands atop the Old Supreme Court; Sir Norman Foster's HSBC building lights up by theme.

Special interest groups pressured the government to seek public opinion on the matter, adding a political nuance during a time when Hong Kong continues to discuss the possibility of direct elections. On hold since 2003, the Central Police Station issue has not been resolved. Neither has the question of democracy.

seat of power

Government House was the official residence and office of 25 British Governors of Hong Kong from 1855 until the handover. Designed in Georgian style with colonial details, it underwent major renovations in the early 1940s while it was used as the military base for the occupying Japanese forces. Since 1997, Hong Kong's Chief Executives have chosen to live elsewhere and reserve the white mansion for special events and entertaining foreign dignitaries.

A short stroll down the hill brings you to St John's Cathedral, the oldest surviving Western church in Hong Kong whose foundation stone was laid in 1847. During the Japanese Occupation, the Anglican church was used as a clubhouse for the Japanese. The Former French Mission building (1917) is located just behind St John's. Distinctive with its green shutters and black wrought-iron details, the neoclassical red brick building is now the Court of Final Appeal. And across the road towards Admiralty is the Flagstaff House Museum of Tea Ware (1846), the oldest existing colonial building in Hong Kong. Built for Major General George Charles D'Aguilar, it was the office and residence of a succession of Commanders of British Forces until 1978.

Closer to the waterfront is the Old Supreme Court. Opened by Governor Frederick Lugard in 1912, it has served as the headquarters for the Legislative Council Chambers since 1985. The elegant old building creates a warm contrast to its sharp, tall neighbours in the heart of the Central business district. Supported by ionic columns, the neoclassical two-storey granite building features a statue of the blindfolded Greek goddess Themis, who represents Justice.

commanding heights

Political dramas are not limited to government offices. Neighbouring bank buildings can also claim their part in the history of Hong Kong. For instance, Sir Norman Foster's design for the Hong Kong and Shanghai Bank (HSBC) building was unveiled during the early days after the handover had been announced. The US$1 billion investment was completed in 1985 and was taken as a sign of HSBC's commitment to remain in Hong Kong for the long term. At the time, the utterly modern appearance of the 179-m (587-ft) headquarters was shocking to many and provoked critics to compare it with Lego blocks. Blurring the line between structural and design elements, the columns and triangular suspension trusses which hold up entire floors are also a distinctive part of the building's exterior image. In the 1980 design brief, the bank requested a flexible interior layout, and Foster responded with a number of high-tech solutions, which included floors and walls made from moveable parts. A 52-m (171-ft) atrium allows visitors to look up into the bank, at the top of which 480 computer-controlled glass mirrors reflect natural light throughout the structure.

The adjacent Bank of China building, constructed after World War II, was subsequently eclipsed in HSBC's shadow. So in the same year, the Bank of China hired Chinese-American architect I.M. Pei to design and build a more impressive structure. To their credit, the earlier art deco building was preserved and an alternative site was found nearby. Inspired by the elegance and strength of bamboo, Pei's twisting geometric design features triangular panels of blue-green glass. The imposing 367-m (1,204-ft) Bank of China Tower—if you include the 50-m (164-ft) 'rugby goal' masts at the top—opened in 1990. Few could miss this message about the future balance of power.

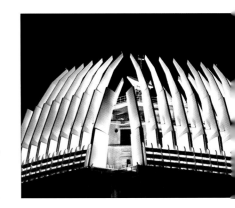

rising to the occasion

Built in 1973, Jardine House is immediately recognisable by its round windows; its 179-m (587-ft) height once made it one of the city's tallest. Formerly known as Connaught Centre, it is now named after one of Hong Kong's most famous tai-pans. It is presently dwarfed by nearby 420-m (1,378-ft) Two ifc (2003). When Two ifc first opened, the Cesar Pelli-designed building bore the world's largest advertisement on a skyscraper that stretched 230 m (755 ft) long.

tall orders

To the east, Central Plaza (1992) in Wan Chai is the next tallest building. At 374 m (1,227 ft) tall, also built on reclaimed land, it is most noticeable for its neon-coloured lights. However, height is not the only way to get noticed in this town.

At the harbour's edge, the Hong Kong Convention and Exhibition Centre extension (1997) is not tall, but its signature curved roof, shaped like the wing of a flying gull or a turtle's back, certainly stands out. It was the site of the official handover in 1997. A few blocks away, the Old Wan Chai Post Office (1915) is the oldest surviving post office building in Hong Kong. Perched near a busy road engulfed in fumes, the pitched-roof structure is, ironically or poignantly, now used as the Environmental Protection Department's Resource Centre.

southern belles

The island's southern district is generally known for its greener pastures, with prime residential properties, more open spaces and better air quality. It is also home to some interesting architectural sites. The Cyberport in Pok Fu Lam is Hong Kong's IT flagship; a campus of around 10 hectares (25 acres) of 'intelligent' offices supported by an IT

THIS PAGE (FROM TOP): The Hong Kong Convention and Exhibition Centre, an iconic structure at the harbour's edge; the Cyberport, the territory's IT flagship.
OPPOSITE (FROM LEFT): The Highcliff and Summit residential towers in Happy Valley; the sharp top of Two ifc.

and telecommunications infrastructure, as well as a five-star hotel, retail and entertainment facilities, and a residential development. In Hong Kong, play the word association game with 'Stanley' and you're likely to hear 'Market', as in the shopping destination (or 'Ho', as in the gambling tycoon). A picturesque place with beaches and housing for the affluent, it is known as Chi Chi Chu in Cantonese ('red pole'), a name which may have come from its silk cotton trees with red blossoms, or from the red sunset of a nearby hill. It also has darker connotations. During World War II, Japanese prisoner-of-war camps were set up here.

The Old Stanley Police Station (1859), the oldest surviving police station in Hong Kong, was the local headquarters for the Japanese gendarmerie. The colonial building was restored to its original purpose after the war and until 1974. Recently, it has been put to commercial use as a restaurant and now, as a supermarket. Through the market and past one of Stanley's beaches is the

expansive, reconstructed Victorian-era Murray House (moved from the current site of the Bank of China Tower in Central). Like a set of antique building blocks, the former British officers quarters was dismantled in 1982 and rebuilt here, brick by brick almost 20 years later. Today, it's a dining and retail hub.

on the waterfront

Across the water, Tsim Sha Tsui in Kowloon evokes bustling streets packed with busy shoppers. However, amidst this retail whirl are reminders of different bygone eras.

as time goes by

The Old Clock Tower is often overlooked as people rush from the Star Ferry Pier to Nathan Road or towards the Hong Kong Cultural Centre and the dome-shaped Hong Kong Space Museum. Dating back to 1915, the clock was part of the former Kowloon-Canton Railway Terminus. It was from here that passengers departed and arrived from what used to be the longest railway journey in the world—Hong Kong to London.

Also in the area, the Former Kowloon British School is the oldest surviving school building. Founded to educate foreign children, its architectural approach resembles that of Victorian-era schools in Great Britain. It now serves as the exhibition gallery of the Antiquities and Monuments Office.

be our guest

The Peninsula is a much-loved building whose history is closely linked with that of Hong Kong. The hotel first received guests in 1928. It was here that the British officially surrendered to the Japanese during World War II, and it was in this lap of luxury

that Japan chose to establish its command during the occupation. The hotel re-opened after the war to once again welcome Hollywood stars, the jet set, and important world figures through its famous doors. The Lobby, a popular meeting place, has seen numerous dramas and intrigues played out under its gilt ceiling. *The New York Times* famously described it as, "a veritable stage-set out of something by Somerset Maugham."

When the hotel announced a renovation plan in the 1960s, it spurred such a reaction that a Society for the Preservation of The Lobby was formed to save it. In 1994, a modern new tower was added with additional rooms, facilities and a restaurant designed by Philippe Starck.

glass houses

The rectangular Hong Kong Observatory in plastered brick sits on a small hill and features arched windows and long verandas on two storeys. Completed in 1883 and declared a monument in 1984, the facility is still used to analyse the weather. The former Marine Police Headquarters compound, built a year later in 1884, is the fourth oldest government facility in existence today. At 1 pm every day until 1907, the time signal tower would drop a time ball to allow ships to check their chronometers. The tower, along with a main building and a stable block, have remarkably evaded Hong Kong's voracious bulldozers.

Jutting out of the skyline directly behind the former Marine Police Headquarters compound, One Peking Road (2003) not only looks good; it does good to the environment too. The 160-m (525-ft) structure, designed by architect Rocco Yim, has a distinctive, curvilinear sail-like façade, creating a visual connection to the curved roof of the Hong Kong Cultural Centre and allowing for environmentally friendly solutions. Solar panels and other features make it possible to reduce the amount of electricity and water used throughout the building's offices and the restaurants on its upper floors. For diners, the breathtaking views are as much of a draw as the cuisine.

THIS PAGE (FROM TOP): One Peking Road with its energy-saving solar panels; engraved stone slabs mark the site of the historical Kowloon Walled City.

OPPOSITE (FROM TOP): Making offerings and burning incense at a temple; huge sandalwood incense coils hang from the ceilings of Man Mo Temple.

if these walls could talk

Amongst the many remnants of traditional structures, none is more notorious or intriguing than Kowloon Walled City. Its history can be traced back to the Sung Dynasty, where it served as an outpost erected to reinforce coastal defence. Large granite slabs were used to construct the city wall with six watch towers and four gateways. Although damaged during the Japanese Occupation, the infamous Walled City became a haven for crooks and drug addicts after the war, and was perceived to be semi-lawless. It was not until 1987 that the government finally swept in to demolish it and set up a park in its place, leaving a few remnants as monuments to the past.

territorial integrity

The sprawling New Territories and outlying islands take up 977 sq km (377 sq miles) or 88 per cent of Hong Kong's total land area. And don't let the name mislead you. The New Territories have some of the oldest structures in the territory, including approximately 40 different declared monuments. Many of them were erected by Hong Kong's five original clans: Tang, Hau, Pang, Liu and Man.

The Tang Ancestral Hall, for example, has been the main ancestral hall of the Tang clan of Ping Shan since it was built about 700 years ago. It is used for celebrations, meetings, festivals and ceremonies. The three-hall building has two internal courtyards. The roofs and main ridges are embellished with Shiwan dragon-fish and pottery unicorns; while the wooden beams are carved with auspicious motifs. Lo Wai Walled village, protected since 1997, is the first walled village built by the Tang clan. Tributes to the spiritual aspect of life were also commissioned by the wealthy, such as Man Mo Temple in the Tai Po area known for its beautiful scenery and wetlands. Tsang Tai Uk ancestral home was built in 1848 by a prosperous stone mason. It was built around five different courtyards and houses

ancestral halls with decorative iron gates and roofs. Located in Yuen Long is one of the most decorative traditional Chinese structures in Hong Kong—the ornate Tai Fu Tai mansion built in Fan Tin village in 1865. The philanthropic Hong Kong Jockey Club assisted in restoring this attractive building in 1988.

island hopping

Signs of early settlements are scattered throughout the outlying islands, including archaeological sites and rock carvings on Cheung Chau and military strongholds on Lantau. Twice the size of Hong Kong Island, Lantau still has a relatively tiny population and was previously best known for the Big Buddha that sits atop one of its many peaks. Only in Hong Kong's recent history have developers turned their eye to this lush island. In the early 1980s, Discovery Bay was created on its east coast as a resort, and has evolved into an alternative residential area with ferry services into town.

up, up and away

When the government sought to expand the airport, Chek Lap Kok off the north shore of Lantau was a natural choice. The airport was moved from Kai Tak in Kowloon, where takeoffs and landings brought passengers close enough to peer inside nearby residential buildings.

Designed by Sir Norman Foster, Hong Kong International Airport is one of the largest of its kind in the world. It's said to have required 6 hectares (15 acres) of glass for its construction, and about 12 hectares (30 acres) of carpeting. An estimated 87 million passengers pass through the airport annually. Although awe-inspiring in itself, visitors are almost more impressed by the rapid train service that speeds travellers to and from the metro areas of Central and Tsim Sha Tsui in less than 30 minutes, and which even allows in-town check-in for most flights.

THIS PAGE (FROM TOP): Hong Kong International Airport at Chek Lap Kok, designed by Sir Norman Foster; the view from the Big Buddha on Lantau island.

OPPOSITE: The Big Buddha sits atop a mountain peak near the Po Lin Monastery.

Twice the size of Hong Kong Island, Lantau still has a relatively tiny population...

Conrad Hong Kong

THIS PAGE (FROM TOP): The grand, lavish lobby is fit for royalty; the entrance into the five-star hotel is equally impressive.

OPPOSITE (FROM LEFT): Feel pampered in the plush settings of the guest rooms; the Deluxe room with harbour view offers a luxurious king-sized bed.

Towering 61 floors above Hong Kong's prestigious retail and entertainment complex Pacific Place, the Conrad Hong Kong is a deluxe, five-star hotel. With direct entry into Pacific Place, it offers unprecedented access to one of the city's most luxurious shopping malls, which contains over 160 designer boutiques and a variety of restaurants. Just 5 minutes in a taxi to the bustling lanes in Central District, a short stroll to the boutiques, galleries and restaurants along Star Street and within walking distance to the famed bars in Wan Chai, the hotel has an enviable location. With such proximity to Hong Kong's major tourist attractions and situated in the heart of the Central Business District, it is a rewarding stay for both businessmen and pleasure-seeking visitors.

The lobby sets the mood for a refined elegance that continues throughout the hotel. Its high ceiling, dramatic hand-painted gold columns and chandeliers set a

...the Conrad Hong Kong is a deluxe, five-star hotel.

grand tone while ornate rugs and antique Chinese furniture add a comfortable, warm touch. Leaving the glow of the reception area, the spacious rooms are equally well-designed with sophisticated, classic features including luxurious bedlinen and gold stencilled wallpaper.

Rooms are well appointed with the latest technology including personal CD player, DVD player and LCD television, high-speed Internet access and satellite television. The elegant accommodations also come with grand marble bathrooms fitted with a deep soaking tub and a separate shower. Each room also shares a stunning view across the Victoria Harbour or the majestic Victoria Peak perched behind chrome skyscrapers.

Surrounded by sightseeing opportunities, tourists can visit the shopping district of Kowloon in just 7 minutes via the city's subway. The Star Ferry sets off from a pier close to the hotel for a harbour tour and a more scenic route across to the mainland. It is easy walking distance to the Peak Tram terminal from where a short, steep climb will take you to some of the most admired views in Asia. Bars, restaurants and shops are scattered around the hotel both eastwards to Wan Chai and westwards to Central.

If you prefer to stay in the hotel, pampering facilities include a fully equipped health club with sauna, steam room, solarium and whirlpool, as well as two spa rooms for

acupressure and aromatherapy massages. Outside, a heated pool set in a lush terrace offers guests sweeping views of the Harbour, a refreshing dip and a relaxing retreat from the city's hustle and bustle. For business travellers, a full-service business centre with private computer stations equipped with high-speed Internet access, mobile phone rental and fully comprehensive secretarial services is available. For large meetings and events, the hotel offers one of the largest ballrooms in Hong Kong, which can cater for up to 1,000 people. So whether you are having a meeting for 10 or a reception for 1,000, the Conrad Hong Kong has the ideal venue to meet your every need.

With restaurants offering everything from superb Italian to exquisite Chinese cuisine, there are some heavyweight enticements for an evening of fine dining within the hotel.

Nicholini's is the only Italian restaurant in Asia to have been awarded the 'Insegna del Ristorante Italiano' by the President of Italy, for being one of the best dining establishments abroad. Similarly, for 13 consecutive years, the *Hong Kong Tatler* has awarded it with its highest accolade as one of Hong Kong's best restaurants. Specialising in northern Italian cuisine with a wide selection of homemade pasta, it is both the exquisite food and cosy, understated décor that does the magic and draws in the crowd. Brasserie on the Eighth

THIS PAGE (FROM TOP): The award-winning Nicholini's serves up classic Northern Italian cuisine amidst cosy settings; indulge in Chinese cuisine with a twist at Golden Leaf.

OPPOSITE (FROM LEFT): The hotel has direct access into Pacific Place; sunbathe upon the terrace and enjoy a relaxing dip in the heated pool.

brings the countryside into the Conrad Hong Kong's urban splendour with some all-time favourite provincial French and continental dishes. With a casual setting and a great wine selection, the restaurant has a laid-back ambience for guests to kick

back and enjoy traditional continental specialities with the freshest ingredients. For some classic Chinese cuisine with a twist, Golden Leaf is the place to visit. Situated at the lobby level with views across the landscaped parklands opposite the hotel, it is outstanding in culinary excellence with both traditional and innovative Chinese food. The extensive menu includes dim sum for lunch and both traditional and modern Chinese dishes from various regions. Garden Cafe overlooks the outdoor pool and offers views across to Kowloon, and offers al fresco dining of barbecue dishes such as freshly grilled ribs, steaks and tasty seafood. With a garden ambience for afternoon tea and unique open-air for evening cocktails, this is an ideal venue for nights of fun without having to step out of the refined Conrad Hong Kong.

FACTS		
ROOMS	513	
FOOD	Nicholini's: northern Italian cuisine • Brasserie on the Eighth: continental cuisine • Garden Cafe: Asian and Western specialities, barbecue • Golden Leaf: exquisite Chinese cuisine	
DRINK	Lobby Lounge • Pacific Bar	
FEATURES	outdoor pool • health club • Grand ballroom and meeting rooms	
BUSINESS	business centre	
NEARBY	Pacific Place • Lan Kwai Fong • Wan Chai Star Ferry • Peak Tram	
CONTACT	Conrad Hong Kong, Pacific Place, 88 Queensway, Hong Kong • telephone: +852.2521 3838 • facsimile: +852.2521 3888 • email: hongkonginfo@conradhotels.com • website: www.ConradHotels.com	

PHOTOGRAPHS COURTESY OF CONRAD HONG KONG.

Four Seasons Hotel Hong Kong

THIS PAGE (FROM LEFT): *Elegant Oriental designs are used in rooms with a touch of traditional Chinese influence; the hotel boasts unsurpassed access to Hong Kong's major commercial and shopping districts.*

OPPOSITE (FROM LEFT): *The marble-clad bathrooms are fitted with lavish amenities; the Presidential Suite comes with an exclusive dining room.*

As the comfortable Airport Express pulls into Central Station half an hour after leaving the airport, most visitors have to decide on additional transport arrangements; but for those staying at the Four Seasons Hotel Hong Kong, your commute ends here.

With direct access to the hotel lobby, where porters are ready to help with your luggage, leaving you free to enjoy and take in the luxury of staying at one of Hong Kong's premier hotels.

Set within one of the four towers of the International Finance Centre (ifc), guests of the Four Seasons Hotel Hong Kong have unsurpassed access to the city's business, shopping and tourist destinations. With its 88-storey tower redefining Hong Kong's skyline, the IFC has become the most prominent and tallest landmark in the city. Thanks to its location, the hotel boasts captivating vistas of the symmetrical structures and the colourful hustle of Victoria Harbour.

Four Seasons Hotel Hong Kong's prestigious address also makes it popular with many multinational companies that reside in offices above ifc mall. In the mall you will find world-renowned retailers sitting alongside some of Hong Kong's most stylish restaurants.

The interior of the Four Seasons Hotel Hong Kong exceeds its world-class reputation with lavish rooms and facilities. In a city where space has long been at a premium, the hotel offers the largest standard rooms, each with a full-length window capturing the best panoramas of Victoria Harbour and Kowloon out to one side and The Peak to the other.

Guests can choose from traditional Chinese décor, which includes authentic brocades and sculpted furniture, or opt for a contemporary Western-style design, with lush silk-panelled walls and marble floors. Bathrooms are generously-proportioned

and stylishly designed with deep marble baths, walk-in rain showers and a built-in LCD TV screen. The Premier and Presidential Suites even come with exclusive dining facilities, enabling visiting VIPs to retain their privacy. These suites also have oversized king bedrooms, a well-equipped pantry and guest powder rooms. All the guest rooms and suites feature high-tech entertainment and work facilities such as high-speed Internet access, DVD players and plasma-screen TV.

Hong Kong is renowned for offering some of Asia's best shopping experiences and an abundance of sophisticated restaurants. Step outside the hotel, take a walk along the steep lanes, and you will come across a slew of antique shops, art

A sanctuary dedicated to luxurious pampering...

galleries, boutiques, bars and restaurants. With the hotel's waterfront location that is adjacent to the famous Star Ferry, you can travel to Kowloon within moments and discover another side of Hong Kong among bustling markets and neon lights. It is hard to ignore the beckoning store displays and tempting offers, so after a hard day of shopping, it will be time to give your tired feet and tensed muscles a rest. At the Four Seasons Hotel Hong Kong, The Spa is the ideal place to do that.

A sanctuary dedicated to luxurious pampering, and one combining state-of-the-art hydrotherapy facilities with a feel of tranquil Asian spirituality, The Spa offers 16 treatment rooms including two exclusive suites, Aqua and Crystal. With their own vitality pool, relaxation day beds, LCD TV and a private bar stocked full of healthy juices and snacks, these spa suites are a calming hideaway where you can completely unwind in peace. Specialising in hydrotherapies, The Spa features an amethyst crystal steam room, an ice fountain for one to cool down in after a visit to the Finnish sauna, tropical steam showers, and a mosaic-tiled vitality pool. Manicure and pedicure lounges have built-in footbaths and a choice of DVDs so while your hands and feet are being pampered, you can kick back in your luxuriant robe

and catch up with Hollywood blockbusters. In the relaxation area, herbal tonics and aromatic waters refresh and rehydrate before an enlivening massage. Treatments include 'Aromatic Odyssey', a deeply relaxing two-hour massage and exfoliation which gives special attention to the face, neck, shoulders and feet. 'Pure Indulgence' uses jojoba pearls, buttermilk, mango butter, honey, sweet orange oil and orange blossom water in a rich and soothing two-hour body and head massage. Other treatments include a silk body massage, peppermint sports pedicure and an invigorating chakra hot oil massage.

The hotel also features a Health Club, pilates studio and oxygenated yoga studio, all with experienced personal trainers. On

the rooftop of the fifth floor, a serene oasis awaits: a lap pool, jacuzzi, plunge pool and a large infinity-edged pool that offers one of the best views in Hong Kong as water flows off towards the breathtaking vistas of Victoria Harbour and Kowloon.

The Pool Terrace restaurant shares the same panorama. You can enjoy a romantic meal under the stars looking out at the city's magical reflection in the water.

For a more formal evening the Four Seasons Hotel Hong Kong hosts two of the city's most formidable restaurants offering French and authentic Cantonese cuisine.

In Caprice you'll find an elegant setting for fine French dining. Sparkling chandeliers light up each table and an open kitchen showcases busy chefs at work

while the enticing aromas of mouth-watering dishes emanate throughout the restaurant. Wild Sea Bass with Pea à la Françoise and Parma Ham and Warm Foie Gras with Pan-Sautéed Butternut Squash and Mango Chutney are just two examples of delicacies guests can expect from the classic menu. Caprice's wine list offers another key attraction: there are over 250 wines, mainly from the Bordeaux and Burgundy regions, and a few exclusive wines from around the world, for discerning customers to choose from.

THIS PAGE (FROM TOP): The breathtaking view that the pool offers; the ice fountain to cool you down after a session in the Finnish sauna.

OPPOSITE (FROM LEFT): Enjoy a luxurious treatment at The Spa; take a dip in the vitality pool.

Lung King Heen, which means 'view of the Dragon', encompasses a modern dining area with timber floors and ceilings, white walls, private booths and, like Caprice next door, great harbour views. A central red column and a 2-m (7-ft) hand-embroidered silk screen dominate the room, giving an Oriental feel to the contemporary design. The food too combines the new with the old, bringing a fresh, light and delicious twist to classic Cantonese cuisine. The beautifully presented dishes include Barbequed Suckling Pig with

THIS PAGE (FROM TOP): Posh and cosy ambience in one of Caprice's private dining rooms; indulge in an exclusive experience at the Chef's Table.

OPPOSITE (FROM LEFT): Enjoy an impressive variety of liquor and creative cocktails; the ultra-cool Blue Bar is the ideal place to have a glass of wine or martini.

For an ultra-modern atmosphere...Blue Bar is the place to be.

Pan-Fried Goose Liver, Baked Crab Shell of Bird's Nest and Crabmeat, and Sautéed Fillet of Garoupa with Matsutake Mushrooms.

For an ultra-modern atmosphere in which guests can chill out with business associates or friends, Blue Bar is the place to be. With brilliant backlit columns and innovative lighting, it is a cool den for light lunches of soups and salads, and is also a perfect setting to end your day with some late evening cocktails. Located on the ground floor on the harbour's edge, its dark, sexy ambience and impressive drinks list make it a superior haunt for viewing Hong Kong's glittering night-time skyline.

FACTS		
ROOMS	399	
FOOD	Lung King Heen: Cantonese • Caprice: French • Lounge	
DRINK	Blue Bar	
FEATURES	spa • 4 outdoor pools • business centre • direct access to Airport Express and ifc mall	
NEARBY	ifc mall • Central • Star Ferry	
CONTACT	Four Seasons Hotel Hong Kong, 8 Finance Street, Central, Hong Kong • telephone: +852.319.688 88 • facsimile: +852.231.968 899 • website: www.fourseasons.com/hongkong	

PHOTOGRAPHS COURTESY OF FOUR SEASONS HOTEL HONG KONG.

Grand Hyatt Hong Kong

THIS PAGE (FROM TOP): *The vast open space of the hotel lobby that leads to the various restaurants; guests can enjoy authentic Italian cuisine at Grissini; boasting the largest pool in Hong Kong, the Grand Hyatt keeps it hidden in lush gardens.*

OPPOSITE: *The minimalist yet sophisticated look of the rooms.*

Grand Hyatt Hong Kong is renowned for its refined atmosphere, its outstanding service and its sophisticated restaurants; and in a city with equal associations, it is one of the best hotel choices. With commanding views of Victoria Harbour, the hotel lies along the waterfront of Wan Chai district. Pacific Place, Admiralty and Central are close by to the west, Causeway Bay lies to its east, and the hotel is just a short walk to the Wan Chai Star Ferry; hotel guests certainly benefit from the easy access to Hong Kong's central business district as well as to the city's most famous shopping and entertainment hubs.

Arriving through the grand art deco entrance, giant black marble pillars stretch up to the ornate ceiling above a galleria level and sweeping staircase. The mosaic floor creates a stunning centrepiece in the lobby, where huge tropical plants bring out a distinctive feel of Asia. The minimalist rooms are less elaborate, though certainly no less sophisticated, with warm wood panelling and wall-to-wall windows that offer spectacular views across the harbour. A huge workstation for business travellers includes a fax and wireless Internet access. There is also a business centre in the hotel to take care of any further requirements.

Eight floors have been appointed exclusively for the Grand Club, where luxurious suites include a private lounge for breakfast, evening cocktails and canapés, and a concierge. There is also access to the hotel's private yacht, Grand Cru. The ultimate luxury, this will definitely impress friends and clients as you cruise around Victoria Harbour and Hong Kong Island.

Organising boat tours, horse racing, water sports, sightseeing tours and even photo processing, the hotel has the most resourceful concierge. Furthermore, it has some of the best recreational facilities. The 50-m (164-ft) outdoor pool—the largest in Hong Kong—is set in a flourishing terrace

garden with views straight out across the harbour so you can enjoy the city's finest panoramas from the luxury of your own sun lounger. If lazing around is not your thing, a jogging track, tennis courts, squash courts and a driving range next door will keep you occupied. Post-exertion, opt for some pampering in Plateau, the hotel's spa.

With revived energy levels, try some of the city's finest cuisine. There are no less than seven restaurants and options include modern Japanese at Kaetsu, Thai and live R&B at JJ's, Cantonese in the stunning setting of One Harbour Road, and al fresco dining at The Grill. Indeed, there is a bounty of choices so you can enjoy your evening in style.

PHOTOGRAPHS COURTESY OF GRAND HYATT HONG KONG.

FACTS		
ROOMS	549	
FOOD	Grand Café: international • Grissini: Italian • JJ's: Thai • Kaetsu: Japanese • One Harbour Road: Cantonese • The Grill: chargrilled specialities by the pool • Tiffin: lunch, tea and dessert buffet	
DRINK	Champagne Bar • JJ's	
FEATURES	spa • outdoor pool • jogging track • tennis • squash • golf driving range • luxury motor yacht • business centre	
NEARBY	Pacific Place • Central • Hong Kong Convention and Exhibition Centre • Star Ferry	
CONTACT	1 Harbour Road, Wan Chai, Hong Kong • telephone: +852.2588 1234 • facsimile: +852.2802 0677 • email: info.ghhk@grandhyatt.com.hk • website: www.hongkong.grand.hyatt.com	

JW Marriott Hotel Hong Kong

THIS PAGE (FROM TOP): *Floor-to-ceiling windows ensure that the exquisite harbour view dominates most areas and rooms—the expansive lobby is a prime example; the modern lines of the hotel's grand exterior.*

OPPOSITE (FROM LEFT): *JW's California restaurant is just one dining option; the hotel can cater for any special occasion.*

Situated between Wan Chai and Central, in the heart of the central business district, Admiralty is fast gaining its own reputation as the most upmarket neighbourhood on the island. As part of the Pacific Place complex in Admiralty, JW Marriott benefits from this exceptional location. With the trendy Star Street nearby, Central a brisk walk away and everything you need within Pacific Place itself, JW Marriott is a perfect base for both business and pleasure. There is also direct access to the mall so you can catch the latest movie and buy everything from golf clubs to gourmet food without even venturing outside.

Rooms are luxurious and combine the modern abstract design of Pacific Place with more traditional Asian art and furniture. Right-angled windows commandeer a dramatic view of either the lush mountains of Hong Kong Island or the bustling Victoria Harbour. Antiques and original artwork throughout the hotel, such as the huge

...rich in history; yet the overriding ambience is one of contemporary comfort.

JW Marriott is credited with five award-winning restaurants; each one refreshingly different. The Fish Bar serves a tantalising fresh catch of the day in a stylishly simple and casual setting featuring wooden beams, fans and open-air sidewalls so diners have uninterrupted views of the harbour. JW's California bears the feel of the West Coast with tall windows and a stark white interior. Asian twists on Californian food and the startling JW's Sushi Bar build a light and tangy menu. For traditional Cantonese, Man Ho Chinese Restaurant offers signature dishes and a seasonal menu in an elegant and authentic setting. The Marriott Café, with remarkable views across the harbour, has an extensive choice of food from around the world—from Indonesian to American classic dishes. What's more, with a Havana-style Cigar Bar, the cosy Book Lounge and the Canton Tea Company serving over 60 choices of hand-selected teas, the distractions are varied and plentiful.

dragon tapestry in the lobby, create an atmosphere rich in history; yet the overriding ambience is one of contemporary comfort.

The hotel's health club offers massages and is equipped with all facilities including a steam room and sauna. Outside, the swimming pool and jacuzzi are surrounded by tropical vegetation. Seven floors up from the bustling streets below, it's a lush oasis with a stunning view of The Peak; a welcoming retreat in this urban jungle.

FACTS		
ROOMS	602	
FOOD	Fish Bar • JW's California and Sushi Bar • Marriott Café • The Lounge • Man Ho Chinese Restaurant	
DRINK	Q88 Wine Bar • Cigar Bar@Q88 • Book Lounge • Canton Tea Company	
FEATURES	outdoor pool • outdoor jacuzzi • health club • stunning harbour views • limousine service	
NEARBY	Central • Admiralty • Wan Chai • Pacific Place	
CONTACT	Pacific Place, 88 Queensway, Hong Kong • telephone: +852.2810 8366 • facsimile: +852.2845 0737 • email: hotel@marriott.com.hk • website: www.marriott.com/HKGDT	

PHOTOGRAPHS COURTESY OF JW MARRIOTT HOTEL HONG KONG.

Le Méridien Cyberport

This ultra-stylish hotel is uniquely located in the south of Hong Kong Island. Attracting businessmen with its high-tech surroundings, and those looking for a peaceful haven away from the throngs of Hong Kong's northern districts—Central, Wan Chai and Causeway Bay—and the bustling streets of Kowloon peninsula, this cyber hotel caters to a fashionable and modern crowd.

Set within the Cyberport Complex, Le Méridien is a part of the architecturally dynamic compound that combines offices, conference space, retail outlets and a host of restaurants and bars. A park of modern chrome, landscaped gardens and wireless connections, the Cyberport Complex and its connected digital city is a staggering US$2 billion project, jetting Hong Kong further into the 21st century. Nestled in the greenery of Telegraph Bay and looking out across the blue waters of the South China Sea, it's a peaceful and architecturally stunning base for business or pleasure.

Everything about the hotel is high-tech, from the 24-hour wireless check-in in the striking reception area to the 'virtual' mini-bar in the guest rooms. Digital cordless phones allow you to roam the grounds and stay in touch; and tablet PCs are also available and can be used by the pool, in the restaurant or in any room thanks to the wireless Internet connectivity throughout the

...visually cutting-edge with full-length windows and stunning ocean views.

hotel. I-pods are available for all guests; and with plasma screens, video-on-demand and intelligent, 'naughty' bathrooms, Le Méridien provides the ultimate state-of-the-art luxuries and is a paradise for any gadget geek.

The rooms too are visually cutting-edge with full-length windows and stunning ocean views. Blissful beds and crisp white linen ensure a good night's sleep, while the ultra-modern lighting and contemporary sofas make watching movies on the huge plasma screen even more enjoyable. Wooden floors, white walls and bright furnishings give the rooms a cool, fresh look. It is, however, the huge glass and chrome bathrooms that set Le Méridien Cyberport above the rest with their outstanding style. Separated from the main living area by a glass wall, this is not an experience for the modest. The oversized, high-pressure rain shower is equipped with a comfortable

bench from where you can watch container ships pass by on the glistening ocean outside while you scrub away the day with some luxurious Hermès shower gel.

Set up for any business event, Le Méridien Cyberport has 16 meeting rooms that seat any number of colleagues from 20 to 300. There's also an auditorium within Cyberport, video-conferencing facilities and an outdoor 'green zone' for business events that include cocktail parties and team building experiences. For those seeking rest,

THIS PAGE (FROM TOP): Nam Fong's millennial décor provides the setting for its delicious and traditional Cantonese food; the lobby greets guests with a highy sophisticated and modern design in which space and light are used to the max.
OPPOSITE: The modern feel flows seamlessly into Bar Umami.

jogging track and fitness centre for the more athletic. Thankfully, a TV is attached to every exercise machine, making it less of a bore. Outside, a pool and neighbouring jacuzzi provide the ultimate sea view; an idyllic and calm haven for you to relax in.

Le Méridien Cyberport has a very comfortable 173 rooms, and incorporates five restaurants and bars spread across the hotel and its gardens. Each one is stunningly designed with exceptional views, stylish lighting and an ultra-cool ambience. Prompt offers an informal setting with outdoor tables and an open-gallery kitchen. Its menu features an eclectic mix of sumptuous Western fare. Bar Umami is a sophisticated Japanese dining bar that's set in a charming outdoor garden and serves a number of

recuperation and a spot of retail therapy, the Arcade, set within the Cyberport Complex, is one of the most innovative shopping malls of its kind. With varying boutiques and restaurants sitting inside this abstract ball of chrome, there are various interactive and multimedia experiences, including a four-screen cinema showing the latest blockbusters alongside independent arthouse movies. Back at the hotel, within the grounds, are a

...stylish lighting and an ultra-cool ambience.

unique temaki, sushi and saketini combinations. For local cuisine the elegant Nam Fong is a superb Cantonese restaurant presented in a funky millennial style. The two bars, Podium (cooking up tantalising tapas) and PSI (serving refreshing cocktails), offer mesmerising sunset views across the ocean; and, later into the night, both are a romantic spot for some star gazing.

With a regular shuttle and limousine service to Central which takes only 15 minutes, there is no need to feel removed from the city's bustling action. With the sound of the ocean, the peaceful dark nights and the abundance of sophisticated restaurants and bars on the doorstep of your room, many guests choose to stay in and dine within the hotel's grounds.

Situated only a short distance from Hong Kong's most famous beach at Repulse Bay, the famed Stanley Market, the surfer's paradise of Big Wave Bay, the idyllic villages and beaches of Shek O, and

surrounded by the beautiful country parks that are just perfect for long walks, Le Méridien Cyberport's superb southern location gives its guests the option of experiencing some of Hong Kong's greatest sites that are often missed during a whirlwind tour of this diverse and green city.

THIS PAGE: PSI bar, for cocktails to watch the sun go down.

OPPOSITE (FROM TOP): A deluxe suite offers all the comforts of home and all the extra conveniences and contemporary style you want from a 21st-century hotel; the ocean view from one of the deluxe suites completes the Hong Kong experience.

PHOTOGRAPHS COURTESY OF LE MÉRIDIEN CYBERPORT.

FACTS		
ROOMS	173	
FOOD	Nam Fong: Cantonese • Prompt: western • Bar Umami: Japanese	
DRINK	Podium: tapas • PSI: cocktails	
FEATURES	outdoor pool • fitness centre • business centre • high-tech environment	
NEARBY	Repulse Bay • Stanley Market • Aberdeen • country parks	
CONTACT	Le Méridien Cyberport, 100 Cyberport Road, Hong Kong • telephone: +852.2980 7788 • facsimile: +852.2980 7888 • email: welcome@lemeridien-cyberport.com • www.lemeridien.com/hongkong	

The Ritz-Carlton, Hong Kong

The Ritz-Carlton, Hong Kong, with its stunning, traditional interior and highly personalised service, is the ultimate choice for classical refinement. Its prime location in the heart of Central gives it unprecedented access, and makes it only a moment's walk, to the boutiques and restaurants in Soho, the antique stores along Hollywood Road and the bars in Lan Kwai Fong. A few blocks from major financial institutions and shopping landmarks, it shares its location with the HSBC building, the Bank of China and the International Finance Centre (ifc Tower); and is just a few steps from the Peak Tram and the world-renowned Star Ferry which offers transport between Hong Kong Island and Kowloon peninsula.

The luxurious guest rooms have uninterrupted views of Victoria Harbour to one side and the dramatic cityscape and The Peak to the other. Enormous beds with grand wooden headboards, delicate antique furniture and enveloping silk armchairs are sumptuous reminders of Hong Kong's opulent past rather than its metallic future. Italian marble bathrooms are lavishly fitted with double sinks, baths and a powerful shower. A Bath Butler is on hand to prepare your bath with candles, flowers and a range of essential oils. Special packages include the 'Evening Out Bath' with peppermint, rosemary and juniper to

invigorate your body while a glass of champagne and chocolate-dipped strawberries will elevate your spirits and ready them for a night out in Hong Kong.

To unwind after an evening out, the Health Club is an intimate retreat equipped with a steam room, sauna and

THIS PAGE (CLOCKWISE FROM TOP): Chic and cosy, The Café is ideal for all-day dining; the romantic and soothing ambience at Toscana; the distinctively European lobby is posh and graceful.

OPPOSITE (FROM LEFT): The elegant one-bedroom suite promises comfort and luxury; the hotel's outdoor pool offers a stunning view of the city.

The Ritz-Carlton, Hong Kong...is the ultimate choice for classical refinement.

state-of-the-art exercise facility. Massage and facial treatments—including the signature Chocolate Facial—pamper and soothe your body and mind. On a smart deck, hemmed in by some of the city's most innovative architecture, an outdoor pool and whirlpool allow you to lie back in style and enjoy the sunshine. For more pressing work matters, you can depend on the secretarial services available to get your work settled on time.

With some of the city's most renowned nightlife playing out on your doorstep, the choices for an enjoyable night out are endless. But if you prefer to spend the evening in the hotel, The Ritz-Carlton, Hong Kong has six outstanding restaurants for you to choose from. Set in a romantic dining room, Toscana serves scrumptious antipasti and pasta dishes that are as refined as the surroundings. The Chater Lounge, a cosy drawing room decorated with exquisite Chinese art, makes for an elegant and relaxing evening with sensuous female vocals. A traditional Cantonese restaurant, Lai Kar Heen, and an art deco-inspired Shanghai-Shanghai serves superb Chinese cuisine; while private tatami rooms in Sakaegawa are perfect for a business lunch or an intimate, romantic dinner.

To help you find time to enjoy the outstanding facilities and restaurants within the hotel, a personal shopper will track down everything from the perfect gift to a Ming dynasty chest, leaving you free for a private speciality bath, a soak in a bubbling outdoor whirlpool, a soothing facial or, as a matter of fact, whatever you would rather do instead.

FACTS

ROOMS	216
FOOD	The Café: continental and Asian • Toscana: Italian • The Chater Lounge • Lai Kar Heen: Cantonese • Shanghai-Shanghai: Shanghainese • Sakaegawa: Japanese
DRINK	Toscana • The Chater Lounge • The Café
FEATURES	outdoor heated pool • health club • bath butler • personal shopper
BUSINESS	secretarial services • audio-visual equipment • Internet access
NEARBY	Star Ferry • ifc Tower • HSBC building • The Landmark • Hong Kong Convention and Exhibition Centre
CONTACT	The Ritz-Carlton, Hong Kong, 3 Connaught Road, Central, Hong Kong • telephone: +852.2877 6666 • facsimile: +852.2877 6778 • email: info@ritz-carlton-hk.com • website: www.ritzcarlton.com

PHOTOGRAPHS COURTESY OF THE RITZ-CARLTON, HONG KONG.

Shama

Shama dominates Hong Kong's serviced apartment scene with its creatively designed and stylish homes. With around 250 units in six locations across Hong Kong Island, Shama now works in partnership with Morgan Stanley; guaranteeing further investment in properties across Asia, beginning with Shanghai.

For those staying longer than a few days, Shama offers a serviced apartment with soul—a more stylish choice with a personal touch. Everything you see in a Shama apartment has been meticulously sourced and selected to give you a feel of home. The staff are pleasingly efficient and discreet; they provide daily cleaning and laundry services, and the friendly concierge can help get you a cab or a table for dinner. Forget lonely nights at the hotel bar and a lack of personal space—a Shama apartment offers a sexy kitchen, dining and lounge area, all of your own, for you to entertain or just relax in.

THIS PAGE (FROM TOP): The sleek lobby of the Mid-Levels apartments; with an excellent use of space and ultimate style, guests can feel instantly at home here.

OPPOSITE (FROM LEFT): A living room in a Causeway Bay apartment; meticulously selected, all details are taken care of by the Shama team who ensure only the best and most stylish for their tenants.

...a serviced apartment with soul...

The fabulous design of Shama Central was created by famous French designer Christian Liaigre, whose impressive portfolio includes the homes of Karl Lagerfeld, Calvin Klein and Rupert Murdoch. There are original artworks on the wall, beautiful hardwood flooring and funky custom-designed furniture—the resulting ambience has been compared to the likes of Ian Schrager and Philippe Starck. The Central and Soho apartments, on Peel Street and Staunton Street respectively, are minutes from the Mid-Levels escalator that motor tirelessly to the Central Business District; a short ramble to the galleries and antique shops along Hollywood Road; and a mere tottering distance to Lan Kwai Fong.

Ten minutes away, the Mid-Levels apartments are perched halfway up The Peak. Its easy access into town and surrounding lush vegetation make this a popular area with expats. Shama in Wan Chai offers a calmer retreat among the lanes off Queen's Road East, near Pacific Place 3; yet within walking distance are the popular restaurants and boutiques of Star Street. Dangerously close to the vibrant shopping complex in Times Square and the Happy Valley Racecourse, Shama's flagship in Causeway Bay offers designer studios and luxury one- and two-bedroom apartments. Roof terraces are divided by ponds and tropical plants with separate dining and barbecue areas. With popular Japanese, Korean and Chinese restaurants in the podium and one of Hong Kong's biggest concentration of bars, restaurants, shops and cinemas on your doorstep, it's a tranquil retreat in a lively neighbourhood.

Offering a platinum gym membership, access to KEE Club, a 'no boundaries' membership card offering copious dining and retail discounts, Shama also helps to set up your social life. With the concierge to show you the way, Shama takes care of a night out as well as a night in.

FACTS

ROOMS	244 apartments over 6 locations
FEATURES	luxurious contemporary designer serviced apartments • high-tech amenities • daily maid service • concierge service • mini complimentary business centre • pet-friendly at Soho and Wan Chai locations • roof terraces • KEE Club • membership to fitness centre
NEARBY	Central • Soho • Mid-Levels escalator • Causeway Bay • Wan Chai • Happy Valley Racecourse • Pacific Place 3
CONTACT	8F Wyndham Place, 44 Wyndham Street, Central, Hong Kong • telephone: +852.2522 3082 • facsimile: +852.2522 2762 • e-mail: info@shama.com • website: www.shama.com

PHOTOGRAPHS COURTESY OF SHAMA.

Plateau Spa

High up on the 11th floor of the Grand Hyatt, in 7,430 sq m (80,000 sq ft) of magnificently designed space, Plateau dedicates itself to aesthetics, relaxation, fitness and culinary excellence. Creating the ultimate sanctuary in central Hong Kong, fountains, pools, waterfalls and lush gardens assure complete tranquillity. Glass walls and granite floors, exuding a refreshing and cooling sense of calm, lead out onto a tree-lined courtyard where a sun terrace and 50-m (164-ft) pool sparkles invitingly. With private pools, glass-walled saunas that overlook the harbour, and some of the most progressive treatments available, Plateau is a luxury spa resort encompassing a full range of five-star services.

To make use of all the facilities and to render yourself completely to the Plateau experience, 14 rooms and suites have been beautifully furnished to offer the finest overnight retreat. Custom-designed futon beds, oversized open jacuzzi baths and rain showers overlooking Hong Kong's cityscape and private terraces are as relaxing as the Plateau's signature massages.

Having been voted as one of the top 25 spas in the world, Plateau's treatments are every bit as luxurious as its surroundings. There are nine dedicated treatment rooms, which provide a much wider license for indulgence. Each treatment is individually tailored to both skin type and mood, and can range from sensual and calming to vigorous and rejuvenating. Traditional detoxifiers, body scrubs, facials, massages, jet lag treatments and pedicures have all been adapted by Plateau to create a unique, sophisticated and personalised

THIS PAGE (CLOCKWISE FROM TOP): For a real indulgent treat, stay in one of the spa suites so you can take full advantage of the facilities around the clock; a quintessentially Hong Kong spa experience—a sauna with a stunning harbour view; the elegance is in the simplicity of a Plateau treatment room.
OPPOSITE: Making full use of the grounds, this treatment room overlooks the water garden.

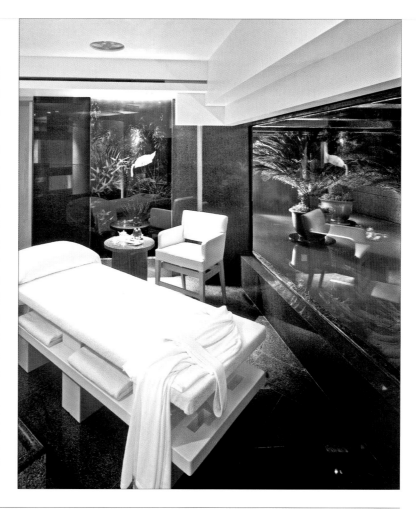

service. Using essential oils, flowers and even semi-precious earth stones to mix the perfect blend to suit each individual, any treatment will leave you positively glowing.

One of Plateau's invigorating signature treatments is an ayurvedic abhyanga-inspired massage that redirects energy into the body. Starting with a rich exfoliating full-body massage, you are then treated to a steam treatment and another massage with cooling body lotion. The unique Vichy Hydro-massage has been crafted to detoxify and intensely relax. A specially designed shower sends pressure point massage jets over the body to stimulate the lymphatic system and release the body's toxins. An aromatherapy massage then soothes you into a state of complete calm.

With its superior treatments and unforgettably soothing environment, you will leave Plateau floating miles above the frenetic bustle and the constant clamour of Hong Kong's hectic life.

PHOTOGRAPHS COURTESY OF PLATEAU SPA.

FACTS

TREATMENTS	massages • facial treatments • scrubs • wraps • manicures • pedicures • reflexology
FOOD	Plateau Courtyard and The Grill
DRINK	Plateau Courtyard and The Grill
FEATURES	14 spa suites • 9 treatment rooms • sauna • steam room • outdoor pool • five fitness and exercise studios • jogging track • gardens • golf driving range • tennis • squash
NEARBY	Pacific Place • Central • Hong Kong Convention and Exhibition Centre • Star Ferry
CONTACT	1 Harbour Road, Wan Chai, Hong Kong • telephone: +852.2584 7688 • facsimile: +852.2584 7738 • email: plateau.ghhk@hyattintl.com • website: www.plateau.com.hk

Star Street in Wan Chai is a popular gathering place for Hong Kong's elite and has quickly gained recognition as an alternative Lan Kwai Fong for Hong Kong's well-heeled community. With fewer bars and a more refined atmosphere, there may be little comparison to Central's bustling hub. However, there is no doubt that if you're looking for a sophisticated night out in Wan Chai, Star Street is the place to go.

Elite Concepts, the owner of 1/5, has played an instrumental role in the development of Star Street and owns several superb restaurants along the street including Cinecittà and One Fifth Grill.

Quite apart from its sister restaurants, 1/5 provides an ultra-cool setting for a night of indulgence and pleasure.

Everything about 1/5 is exclusive, including the discreet entrance that you'll find on a narrow side street. Climbing the stairs and venturing over a small bridge, you arrive at the top floor of the multi-level bar. From here, on a dramatic marble platform, you gain a stunning aerial view of the whole bar. Heavy wood and dark leather furniture sit smartly alongside timber and concrete architecture. Spectacularly high ceilings, full glass windows and glittering lights create an impressive backdrop. Low, intimate booths

THIS PAGE (FROM TOP): *With this much selection, challenge a bartender to any cocktail and 1/5 will undoubtedly rise to it; cosy and laid-back yet modern and cool, the stylish charm keeps customers coming back.*

OPPOSITE (FROM LEFT): *Soft lighting completes the ambient décor; if your evening calls for some privacy, there are many nooks and crannies to suit your needs.*

...an ultra-cool setting for a night of indulgence.

visitors to Hong Kong. Yet, despite its 'celebrity hangout' status, 1/5 remains pleasingly down to earth. Regular events add a sense of fun to the bar; and while a 'Spa Sunset' (including free manicures) might entice the ladies, 1/5 relies on its solid selection of alcohol to bring in the men.

Renowned also for its music, 1/5 attracts international DJs to its intimate venue playing R&B and down tempo house. However, this underground glamour bar is more a place to sip designer drinks—signature cocktails include Pink Lemonade, Lychee Caprioska and Alice in Wonderland—and listen to the chill-out vibes than an arena to show off your steps on the dance floor.

The bar's clever name refers to the missing fifth of the 4/5 quart bottle used in the United States. With the emphasis on relaxed sophistication, friendly service and great cocktails, it is difficult to find anything missing from 1/5.

and varying raised lounge areas offer privacy while a dark oak bar caters for a more informal setting. A cool room behind the bar works as a showcase for the immense number of bottles that 1/5 stocks—a huge and diverse variety of spirits, champagnes, wines and beer.

This chic New-York-style setting attracts an equally sophisticated crowd and draws in upmarket expatriates and prestigious

SEATS	140
DRINK	cocktails • wine • champagne • spirits
FEATURES	guest DJs • special events • private room
NEARBY	Wan Chai • Pacific Place, Admiralty
CONTACT	9 Star Street, Wan Chai, Hong Kong • telephone +852.2520 2515 • facsimile +852.2596 0283 • email: 1/5@elite-concepts.com • website: www.elite-concepts.com

Cinecittà

Hong Kong's love affair with Italian food is a time-tested one and, second only to Chinese, it's undoubtedly a favourite cuisine. As with many cities around the world, Hong Kong has many choices when looking for the food of love; however for truly authentic flavours and wonderful settings there is just a handful to recommend.

Cinecittà is one such place that stands high above the rest. Named after the fabled film studio where the great films of Fellini and Vittorio de Sica were created, it stays true to its identity with large prints of Fellini films adorning the walls. The restaurant is modern and stylish, made up of a stunning glass frontage and metal canopy. The sleek interior is defined by a further abundance of glass that creates sharp lines and a mirage of reflections yet, on a practical level, helps split the room into sections. Along one side a striking glass walk-in wine cellar stocks interesting wines from every wine region of

THIS PAGE (FROM TOP): *Calming lighting and lush drapes create an air of luxury and warmth allowing you to completely relax as you enjoy some classic Italian cuisine; the glass walk-in wine cellar is an impressive sight.*

OPPOSITE: *Cinecittà's discreet private dining room is the ideal setting for a celebratory dinner or business lunch.*

...the food at Cinecittà surpasses its stunning surroundings.

Italy. The starkness of its shell and razor-sharp angles are softened by the beautiful mosaic ceiling, rich terracotta tones and rustic, wooden furniture.

Serving exquisite classic Italian dishes with tasty pastas, crisp salads and delicious seafood, the food at Cinecittà surpasses its stunning surroundings. The appetising menu includes Parma ham filled with Mozzarella or Baked Butter Mushrooms, Roasted Rack of Lamb with crusted hazelnut, and 'Bigoli' with Duck Ragoût and Porcini. On the list of desserts, which includes the refreshing sorbets and ice-creams, is a sinful bitter Chocolate Flan with Banana Ice-cream. For a lighter lunch, Cinecittà also encompasses an antipasto bar where you can enjoy drinks, snacks and canapés in their weekly happy hour. An outside terrace sets the tone for a more leisurely meal where diners can take in the Wan Chai buzz over some pasta and a glass or two of crisp Italian white wine.

Owned by Elite Concepts, Cinecittà was one of the first restaurants to open on Star Street, a popular nightspot area increasingly recognised for its upmarket bars and restaurants. The restaurant's huge success over the last six years has led the

way in transforming Star Street from a little known back street in Wan Chai to the latest hangout for Hong Kong's in-crowd. Its convenient location off of Queen's Road East makes it a quick and easy stroll from Pacific Place and Central.

FACTS

SEATS	100
FOOD	Italian
DRINK	Italian wine
FEATURES	outside terrace • antipasto bar • wine cellar
NEARBY	Wan Chai • Pacific Place, Admiralty
CONTACT	Cinecittà, 9 Star Street, Wan Chai, Hong Kong • telephone: +852.2529 0199 • facsimile: +852.2529 5399 • email: cin@elite-concepts.com • website: www.elite-concepts.com

FINDS

FINDS, an acronym for Finland, Iceland, Norway, Denmark and Sweden, could just as easily stand for fantastically innovative, and naughtily delicious Scandinavia, yet whatever its true meaning there is no doubt that this Nordic collective is one of the coolest spots in Hong Kong.

Inspired by the icy-cold winters of Scandinavia, FINDS's interior is totally refeshing—as unique as a snowflake. The lift door opens onto the bar and restaurant and you're immediately struck by an expanse of tiny lights, glistening white surfaces and a huge turquoise banquette jutting from the slate floor like an iceberg. Dominating this startling space, an enormous, sparkling chandelier cascades towards the floor. Along one side, bartenders serve Aquavit and Koskenkorva from behind a smooth, curved bar. For those inclined, celebrity cocktails such as a Greta Garbo or an Ingmar Bergman are also mixed on demand. At the end of the restaurant an unusually large terrace looks out across the bustling Lan Kwai Fong area.

Unlike its frosty design, FINDS has a warm and lively atmosphere. In true Scandinavian form, behind the image-conscious façade is a down-to-earth and friendly charm that has not gone unnoticed in Hong Kong. Lunchtime is buzzing with businessmen rushing in and out; those with

...this Nordic collective is one of the coolest spots in Hong Kong.

more time to spare recline in the sunshine on the terrace; and crowds celebrate with another shot of vodka. At night-time the lively restaurant slips into a late night bar and lounge where, until the early hours, cocktails and champagne cater to a sophisticated set of locals, expats and tourists.

While David Buffery has created a dazzling arctic summer with his interior design, Chef Jaakko Sorsa adds the Northern Lights with his truly innovative cuisine. Their scapas—Scandinavian tapas—provide the perfect bar snack. The Smoked Salmon Mousse is a superb accompaniment to a Cucumber Martini, while some Finnish Meatballs can be washed down with a shot of Stoli. The main dining menu combines regular favourites such as Buckwheat Blinis with Lavaret Roe and Sour Cream with more unusual dishes including Tender Venison with a Blackcurrant Sauce. The restaurant imports seasonal fresh food; a comforting Wild Mushroom Broth with Poached Eggs and Ham is a great winter warmer while the tangy Lemon Gravalax with Potato Salad and Artichoke Crème Brûlée with Potato Pancakes are deliciously light and certainly call for a chilled glass of white on the terrace. The presentation is impeccable and in such a stunning environment, the dishes live up to this wonderfully creative flair. But overall, it's the fun, cheeky character behind the haute-design that makes FINDS a real find. Kippis!

THIS PAGE (FROM TOP): Those just out for a drink can enjoy cocktails at the bar; well thought out design makes FINDS a unique hotspot.

OPPOSITE: As you enter, FINDS's Nordic detail will transport you far from Hong Kong to the land of the Northern Lights.

FACTS		
SEATS	restaurant: 80 • bar/lounge: 90	
FOOD	modern Scandinavian	
DRINK	extensive wine list • champagne • cocktails	
FEATURES	casual fine dining • outdoor terrace • late night bar and snacks • private parties	
NEARBY	Central • Lan Kwai Fong	
CONTACT	2nd Floor LKF Tower, 33 Wyndham Street, Central, Hong Kong • telephone: +852.2522 9318 • facsimile: +852.2521 9818 • email: reservations@finds.com.hk • website www.finds.com.hk	

JJ's

If you're searching for Hong Kong's top celebrity hangout then you should head straight to JJ's. Situated on the ground floor of the Grand Hyatt, this sassy club-style bar overlooks Victoria Harbour in the Wan Chai District. Both a musical institution and stylish restaurant, JJ's recently went under the knife of Hong Kong-based American architect John Morford, whose previous designs include the Park Hyatt Tokyo, made famous by Sofia Coppola's award-winning film *Lost In Translation*. With JJ's sleek new smoky black look and lively ambience, Bill Murray's lonely character should have come here for a drink instead.

Although perched on the upper level, JJ's Music Bar has a cosy atmosphere like that of a small New York Club. The walls are cluttered with black-and-white photographs of iconic musicians—of which some of the more recent have been known to visit JJ's to listen to the mix of soul, rhythm

THIS PAGE (FROM TOP): The dining room keeps a contemporary edge with clean white tables that contrast against the dark walls; the intimate Back Bar where you can sit back and drink while taking in the sounds from the live band in the Music Room.

OPPOSITE: The cosy Wine Room, featuring six private booths and a huge selection of international wines on proud display.

and blues. Dark suede banquettes and leather stools all point towards the stage where the resident band, *WJ and the Tonemasters*, entertains with a mix of their own songs and a great selection of covers. Collectively it is possibly the most seasoned band playing out of Hong Kong, having toured alongside some of the most renowned jazz and R&B artists including platinum-selling soul diva Oleta Adams, Lenny Kravitz and Beyonce.

From the Music Room, the sophisticated surroundings continue into the Lounge and Back Bar. Overlooking the restaurant, it's an open area where guests can enjoy cocktails prepared by top mixologists.

Below, the Dining Room resumes the sultry sleek look of the Music Bar with dark steel pillars, glass walls looking out onto the hotel's reception area and funky, art deco seating. Sparkling white tables keep the restaurant entirely modern and cool; and, in contrast with the minimalist feel, the food is informal, home-style Thai cooking with truly authentic flavour. Chef Khun Siriluck, a celebrity in Thailand, grew up inspired by the dishes her grandmother made in the Thai Royal kitchens. Adding regional twists and an exciting range of spices and herbs, her family-style cuisine has also served the Thai Royal Family. An unlikely combination of R&B and Thai, JJ's relaxed and fun ambience really makes it a pleasant surprise.

FACTS

SEATS	dining: 88 • Music Room: 150
FOOD	Thai
DRINK	international wine list • Music Room: cocktails • martinis
FEATURES	live R&B • great atmosphere
NEARBY	Wan Chai • Pacific Place • Central • Hong Kong Convention and Exhibition Centre • Wan Chai Star Ferry
CONTACT	1 Harbour Road, Wan Chai, Hong Kong • telephone: +852.2584 7662 • facsimile: +852.2824 2060 • email: jjs.ghhk@hyattintl.com • website: hongkong.grand.hyatt.com

PHOTOGRAPHS COURTESY OF JJ'S.

KEE Club

KEE Club was conceived by a group of friends who brought together their own experiences and inspiration: from an inherent knowledge of fine cuisine, being part of one of Hong Kong's most historic gourmet Chinese restaurants; from parties influenced by stories of great masquerades in Austria; from exposure to music that makes a club a success; from indepth family knowledge of cinematic art, and from generations of exposure to classic and contemporary art in Europe and Asia.

This Private Members' Club, situated above the famous Yung Kee goose restaurant, is a place where friends can gather to appreciate outstanding cuisine, fine wines, great music and art—the good life. Today, KEE Club is recognised as one of Hong Kong's most sophisticated yet fun meeting places, and has become renowned for throwing parties for celebrities such as The Rolling Stones, Sting and Michael Jordan. Its membership card is a must-have for the city's elite. KEE extends its hospitality to out-of-towners through a special arrangement with select five-star hotels whose guests are allowed access if booked in advance by the hotel's concierge.

The club's interior is inspired by an eclectic mix of European luxury, New York chic and African and Asian bohemia. Dappled in natural light by day and cast with long shadows from candlelight by night, it exudes a refined, seductive atmosphere, with a dark bar, Jacobsen's Swan & Egg chair and

THIS PAGE (FROM TOP): The plush salons are perfect for private parties and intimate meetings; the gilt staircase leading up to the Venetian Dining Room.

OPPOSITE (FROM LEFT): Appreciate beautiful works of art amid stylish settings; the dark, sultry bar serves up creative cocktails and premium wines.

Centurion Salons, each can be transformed to cater to confidential business deals, backgammon championships or private parties. In the lavishness of the Venetian Dining Room, with the glamour of a Venetian Palazzo, KEE Club serves up some of Hong Kong's finest dim sum over an intimate lunch. At dinner, Head Chef Bonelli, whose training has taken him into the kitchens of the world's best restaurants including El Bulli in Spain and The Fat Duck in England, creates outstanding menus of sublime and contemporary cuisine. House specialities include Boston Lobster & Goose Liver.

With one of the city's most prestigious wine cellars and a diverse list of house cocktails, the KEE Club is one of Hong Kong's hottest venues for hosting big-ticket events and hip parties with top international DJs and entertainers.

a dramatic open inner staircase leading to the Venetian Dining Room. Decked with paintings, sculptures and antiques collected by the owners on their travels around the world, you can appreciate works by artists and designers as prominent as Picasso, Topor and Starck.

On the lower floor there is a bar and lounge that can also be used as a private screening room, used for film festivals and private shows; and three intimate salons, each with their own distinct décor and ambience. From the peaceful Purple salon that doubles up as a library to the opulent Red and

FACTS

FOOD	contemporary Italian • Cantonese
DRINK	extensive wine list • cocktails
FEATURES	exclusive private member's club (concierges at select five-star hotels can arrange access) • restaurant • lounge bar • private salons • library • screening room • DJs • events • extensive art collection
NEARBY	Lan Kwai Fong • Star Ferry • Victoria Peak • Victoria Harbour • Central shopping and business area
CONTACT	6th Floor, 32 Wellington Street, Central, Hong Kong • telephone: +852 2810 9000 • facsimile: +852 2868 0036 • email: info@keeclub.com • website: www.keeclub.com

PHOTOGRAPHS COURTESY OF KEE CLUB.

Lan Kwai Fong

In the early 1980s, Allan Zeman—regarded as the 'King of Lan Kwai Fong'—opened California on D'Aguilar Street. Its immediate success prompted huge growth around the tiny street in Central, and now a warren of over 100 bars and restaurants make Lan Kwai Fong one of the most happening bar districts worldwide.

The atmosphere is at quietest, rowdy; and at loudest, a carnival of immense scale. Every day crowds surge from the mass of open fronted bars, music spills into the air, and a mass of neon lights direct eager punters to the bar. Party revellers make their way here to enjoy some of the city's best nightlife, making it a must on any to-do list during a Hong Kong trip.

Next to the ever flourishing California is the more recent Lux Restaurant and Bar which, for three years, has been host to some of the hippest visitors to Lan Kwai

Fong. Dominated by a central, circular bar serving some of the area's best cocktails, Lux is a popular haunt for those seeking something a little more sophisticated. Transforming into a dance club late into the night with a host of resident DJs, Lux progresses from a candlelit refuge for intimate drinking to a great party for late-night dancing—a sure guarantee after a few cocktails. Lux further combines as a stylish restaurant with a Mediterranean-influenced menu. The cuisine is simple and contemporary, offering a great selection of steaks and seafood.

Renowned as much for its varied eateries as its wild partying atmosphere, Lan Kwai Fong offers a diverse choice of award-winning restaurants from French cuisine at the elegant Café des Artistes to Japanese at

THIS PAGE (CLOCKWISE FROM TOP LEFT):
The sushi bar at Kyoto Joe immediately captures you with its striking blue walls and modern rice paper lanterns; during the daytime, Lux is a relaxing spot for a quiet lunch; while at night, Lux transforms into the pumping heart of Lan Kwai Fong's scene.
OPPOSITE: Combined with great food, the Japanese décor brings an air of authenticity.

the modern and sleek Kyoto Joe. In Asia's fast-moving market, Café des Artistes has long been one of Hong Kong's finest French restaurants serving mouth-watering dishes. Located on the first floor, surrounded by breezy open windows overlooking the bustling street below, Café des Artistes offers a relaxed and serene ambience rarely found in Central, and is the perfect setting to watch the madness of Lan Kwai Fong while you enjoy your wine in the calm.

Japanese food lovers should not miss Kyoto Joe. The restaurant is divided into a sake bar that opens out onto the street; a robata yaki bar, where the finest meats are grilled in front of you; and a great sushi bar with dramatic blue, backlit walls. Whether an evening of fine wine and creative cuisine in intimate, private rooms or quick stop for a light snack or bottle of sake at the bar, Kyoto Joe caters to all aspects of Hong Kong life and is certainly one of the cool kids on the Lan Kwai Fong block.

PHOTOGRAPHS COURTESY OF LAN KWAI FONG.

FACTS

SEATS	Lux: 62 • Café des Artistes: 80 • Kyoto Joe: 60
FOOD	Lux: Mediterranean • Café des Artistes: French • Kyoto Joe: Japanese
DRINK	Lux: cocktail bar • Kyoto Joe: sake bar
FEATURES	fine dining • great atmosphere
NEARBY	Lan Kwai Fong • Central District • Star Ferry
CONTACT	UG/F., California Tower, 30-32 D'Aguilar Street, Central, Hong Kong • Lux: telephone: +852.2868 9538 • facsimile: +852.2869 9510 • Café des Artistes: telephone: +852.2526 3880 • facsimile: +852.2147 3456 • Kyoto Joe: telephone: +852.2804 6800 • facsimile: +852.2804 6030 • email: info@lkfgroup.com • website: www.lkfe.com

Lotus Restaurant

A checklist for the ultimate night out in Hong Kong should include a menu from a top international chef, bountiful cocktails, ultra-hip surroundings in an up-to-the-minute location, and a DJ pumping chilled sounds to the crowd. With sophisticated restaurants, late night bars and various entertainment districts, Hong Kong provides you with many options for such a night out; however, to avoid an intermittent evening of taxis, queues and membership cards, Lotus ticks all these boxes in just one location with its dusk-until-dawn celebrations.

On a narrow lane in Central, next to the bars, restaurants and boutiques of Soho, and minutes from the crowds of Lan Kwai Fong, Lotus is located in a hotspot for Hong

Kong's young and fashionable. Inside, the dining area is separated by stunning carved teak panels, which are backlit to brilliant effect. On the other side the bar stretches through to an outside terrace where revellers can spill out onto the street. Everything about Lotus dictates cool, understated sophistication; yet the ambience is pleasingly relaxed and casual. The interior is a retro blend of earthy tones and textures; the sexy seating area includes 1960s-style red leather armchairs; and the bar dominates with its sleek and unique shape. Open for lunch and dinner all week, at weekends Lotus continues into the night as a late lounge with top local and international DJs.

The food is as inventive as the décor, with renowned Australian chef Will Meyrick in charge of the menu. Continuing in an Asian theme from his famous Thai Restaurant, Jimmy Liks in Sydney, Chef

THIS PAGE (FROM LEFT): The lounge where the Lotus crowd can kick back and experience the unique cocktails of celebrity mixologist, Grant Colllins; a fresh and inspired Asian-style dish from Chef Will Meyrick.

OPPOSITE: Combining retro-elements with classic style, the panels shield the dining area, keeping it relaxed and intimate.

...cool, understated sophistication...

Meyrick has been inspired from food across Southeast Asia, in particular Thailand and Indonesia, to create some exciting and delicious varieties. Signature dishes include a light and fresh Salad of Crispy Salmon with Water Melon, Ginger, Thai Basil and Chilli Dressing, and a mouth-watering Vietnamese Braised Rib Beef with Mint Thai Basil and a Tangy Hot and Sour Salad.

The art of drinking is an important pastime in Hong Kong; and Lotus has literally raised the bar with the introduction of cocktail mixologist, Grant Collins. Having shaken concoctions in top bars around the world, Collins is now bringing the new generation of cocktails to Hong Kong. The list of tantalising drinks is seemingly endless with Charred Lime and Ginseng Daiquiris, Blueberry and Vanilla Mojitos, and the signature Lotus Martini making up for just a drop of gin in a tonic ocean. This is certainly not the bar to challenge your way up to the top shelf; it would be an impossible task.

FACTS

SEATS	dining: 70 • cocktails: 200 • VIP area: 20
FOOD	modern Asian
DRINK	cocktails
FEATURES	outside terrace • cocktail mixologist • regular DJs
NEARBY	Central • Soho • Lan Kwai Fong
CONTACT	37–43 Pottinger Street, Central, Hong Kong • telephone: +852.2543 6290 • facsimile: +852.2541 6588 • Email: info@lotus.hk • website: www.lotus.hk

One Fifth Grill

Once a burrow of seedy streets and knocking shops, Wan Chai—the famed red-light district of Hong Kong—is now opening up into a voguish extension of Central. With Pacific Place housing heavyweight five-star hotels and the nearby Star Street springing into life with a row of fashionable bars and restaurants, there's a new place in town for Hong Kong's chic set.

A more recent addition to the growing number of chic restaurants on Star Street is one fifth grill, whose owner, Elite Concepts, has played an instrumental part in the development of the area. The restaurant is a celebration of contemporary European style that features deep booths and banquettes, stunning high ceilings and a lively, open kitchen—one fifth grill is the epitome of casual chic. Wooden pillars, mellow lighting and an emanating orange glow meld together to create an inviting, rustic warmth, heightened by the intimacy of the small main dining area. Far from rustic in style however are the trendy urban sets often found here discussing business deals or sampling the signature aperitifs. Chattering

...one fifth grill is the epitome of casual chic.

lunch-time diners and sophisticated evening lovelies give one fifth grill an exclusive reputation that makes pre-booking essential.

Walking through an impressive glass-encased wine cellar on arrival and venturing straight to the aperitif bar, you'll soon discover one fifth grill is well-stocked in everything from biodynamic wines to classic aperitifs such as Pastis, Kir Royal and Negroni. With a somewhat colonial feel, the bar itself creates a great setting for pre-dinner cocktails or a passing beer.

As its name suggests, the focus here is on the grill in European style, which stresses on the absolute best quality and emphasises on seafood and prime cuts of meat including Grilled Sea Bass, Salmon Steak, Lamb Chops and Sirloin Beef. Its sauces are truly mouth-watering, with a variety of unique creations that add an exciting flavour such as Béarnaise, Truffle Sauce, Rosemary and Lime Gravy, Chimichurri Salsa and Citrus Butter.

There's an understated sophistication to one fifth grill that makes it both relaxed and convenient for a quick drink after work; and exciting and special for a celebratory or romantic night out. With 1/5 drawing you in next door, complete your evening of biodynamic fine wine with some of Hong Kong's finest cocktails.

THIS PAGE: Defying the 'fine dining' label, diners will find one fifth grill suitable for business clients or friends.

OPPOSITE (CLOCKWISE FROM TOP): You can enjoy a pastis at the aperitif bar; now an institution on Star Street, one fifth grill's stylish décor is immediately apparent; the carefully selected wines are kept in the superb cellar.

FACTS

SEATS	86
FOOD	European grill
DRINK	classic aperitifs • biodynamic wine
FEATURES	wine cellar • bar
NEARBY	Wan Chai • Pacific Place, Admiralty
CONTACT	9 Star Street, Wan Chai, Hong Kong • telephone: +852.2529 6038 • facsimile: +852.2596 0283 • email: ofg@elite-concepts.com • website: www.elite-concepts.com

PHOTOGRAPHS COURTESY OF ONE FIFTH GRILL.

One Harbour Road

Rated as one of the city's best hotel restaurants, One Harbour Road combines the finest traditional Cantonese food with a stylish environment. Located on the seventh and eighth floors of the Grand Hyatt in Wan Chai, a glass elevator delivers you straight from the lobby to the restaurant where sweeping views stretch out across Victoria Harbour.

Inspired by a 1930s taipan mansion, the restaurant has a romantic colonial feel. Marble balustrades separate private dining areas; trees potted in vast Chinese pottery offer imaginary shade; and, from the galleria above, hanging baskets overflow with ivies and flowers. The central lotus pond and a background sound of gentle running water evoke tranquillity you cannot find in any other Cantonese restaurant. With a glass roof allowing sunlight to flood across the restaurant and floor-to-ceiling windows looking out across the harbour you can enjoy some of Hong Kong's finest traditional cuisine in a glorious conservatory setting.

While other restaurants modernise Cantonese food with fusion twists, One Harbour Road stays true to the traditional recipes by creating a variety of unpretentious tasty dishes. With Pan-Fried Bird's Nest in Scrambled Eggs, Double-Braised Shark's Fin with Bamboo Piths and Braised Abalone with Oyster Sauce on the menu, you can sample all the renowned dishes from the

...tranquillity you cannot find in any other Cantonese restaurant.

Where traditional Cantonese restaurants are raucous, tightly packed halls with heavy décor, One Harbour Road has created somewhere elegant and private to enjoy Cantonese food. With light streaming through the roof and a picturesque split-level dining room, it is certainly worthy of its reputation as the best of its kind.

southern China region. However, One Harbour Road also excels in lesser-known local specialities. Crispy Eel Tossed in Cinnamon Flowers, Chilli Prawns with Lychee and Sugar Peas, Deep-Fried Crab in its Shell, and Wok-Fried Scallops are all cooked to perfection, melting in a delightful blend of flavours. You cannot go to a Cantonese restaurant without trying dim sum; and here you will find bundles of joy delivered to your table in the form of fluffy dumplings and crispy spring rolls.

PHOTOGRAPHS COURTESY OF ONE HARBOUR ROAD.

FACTS

SEATS	212	
FOOD	Cantonese	
DRINK	international wine list • Chinese tea	
FEATURES	conservatory style • stunning views • lotus pond	
NEARBY	Wan Chai • Pacific Place • Central • Hong Kong Convention and Exhibition Centre • Wan Chai Star Ferry	
CONTACT	1 Harbour Road, Wan Chai, Hong Kong • telephone: +852.2584 7938 • facsimile: +852.2824 2060 • email: info.ghhk@hyattintl.com • website: www.hongkong.grand.hyatt.com	

Yè Shanghai

Embracing the decadence and heady atmosphere of Shanghai in its 1930s heyday, yè shanghai looks dark, sexy and glamorous; it stands as a stunning backdrop for sampling some of the finest Shanghainese cuisine on the island. With restaurants on either side of Victoria Harbour, in Tokyo and in its mother city Shanghai, an evening at yè shanghai is definitely a unique experience and one that can be enjoyed at a growing number of locations.

Far removed from the cluster of the average Chinese restaurant, yè shanghai—translating directly as 'Shanghai nights'—is stylish and elegant. While one part of it celebrates Shanghai's dazzling past as the 'Paris of the East' with original art deco leather armchairs and live jazz; another ensures the overwhelming feel is contemporary and fresh with huge airy windows, chrome lighting and a fusion twist on traditional Shanghainese cuisine.

THIS PAGE (FROM TOP): Crispy turnip cakes, a traditional treat during Chinese New Year, are served all year at yè shanghai; the stylish corridor at the Kowloon restaurant.

OPPOSITE (FROM LEFT): Although style is important, the comfort of diners is not compromised; for after-dinner drinks, you can retire to the bar for a cocktail.

...yè shanghai looks dark, sexy and glamorous...

The provinces of Jiangsu, Zhejiang and Shanghai make up the Shanghainese culinary umbrella. On the menu you'll find Steamed Pork Dumplings, Deep Fried Sweet and Sour Yellow Fish with Pine Nuts and Hairy Crabs, all indicative of the region. More unusual are the desserts such as the Black Sesame Crème Brûlée with Roasted Peanut Ice-Cream, Mango Napolean and Tofu Bavarian with Blueberry Compote and Ladyfingers.

The original yè shanghai opened in Pacific Place in Admiralty on Hong Kong Island in 1998. Among the glimmering metal and mirrored glass of Pacific Place, a mass of 21st-century chrome that houses an elite shopping mall, five-star hotels and a high-tech office space, yè shanghai dedicates itself to another era—one of jazz, glamour and fascination. And with a floor-to-ceiling mirror, musicians on the raised stage and lively diners dancing on the dance floor the atmosphere is indeed enchanting.

Across the water in Kowloon, a second yè shanghai is located only minutes from the Star Ferry Pier in the Marco Polo Hongkong Hotel. Entering through a wrought-iron gate, the main dining room and bar stir up an immediate sense of art deco, a style that overtook Shanghai more than any other city in the 1930s. With such design consideration the atmosphere is always intimate, sensuous and glamorous with retro booths, red walls, floor lamps and paintings by Macau's Fernanda Dias. For a little privacy, be it a discreet business meal, a celebration or a romantic dinner, the private dining rooms open onto a stunning veranda and bamboo garden from where you can admire Victoria Harbour's view and the dazzling lights of Hong Kong Island.

FACTS

SEATS	Hong Kong: 170 • Kowloon: 190
FOOD	Shanghainese
DRINK	wine • cocktails
FEATURES	retro atmosphere • live jazz
NEARBY	Pacific Place: Admiralty • Hong Kong
	Marco Polo Hongkong Hotel: Tsim Sha Tsui • Kowloon
CONTACT	Pacific Place: Level 3, Pacific Place, Hong Kong • telephone +852.2918 9833 • facsimile +852.2918 0651 • e-mail: ysh@elite-concepts.com
	Kowloon: 6/F Marco Polo Hongkong Hotel, Kowloon, Hong Kong • telephone +852.2376 3322 • facsimile +852.2376 3189 • e-mail: ysk@elite-concepts.com • website: www.elite-concepts.com

PHOTOGRAPHS COURTESY OF YÈ SHANGHAI.

Barney Cheng

Over Barney Cheng's glamorous and exotic life he has exhibited his bold designs alongside some of the world's most prominent designers, including Vera Wang, Vivienne Tam and Giorgio Armani. His commissions and partnerships over the years have been no less prestigious and include a diverse selection of celebrated names and esteemed brands such as Harry Winston, HSBC and Jaguar. For DeBeers, he designed a lavish bridal collection, the highlight of which was a wedding gown encrusted with over 550 diamonds totalling 100 carats and valued at an amazing HK$2 million. In 1999 he became the first designer to create an exclusive line for Marks & Spencer, named 'The Comfort Zone' which became available throughout Southeast Asia. His famously dazzling fashion shows have been held across the globe from the Forbidden Palace in Beijing with Longines watchmakers to Los Angeles with Giorgio Beverly Hills.

THIS PAGE (FROM TOP): Providing an intimate and relaxed space for customers to browse through designs and fabrics, Barney Cheng's bridal salon is a one-stop shop for brides-to-be.

OPPOSITE: Whether it's a knock-out creation or a more casual affair, the clothing range displays Cheng's innate sense of style and creativity.

Creating new trends in Hong Kong, he uses unique textures, fabrics and colours...

With such dynamic, fantastical designs it is no surprise that Cheng attracts such venerated company and has become a favourite among celebrities. He has designed Oscar dresses for Michelle Yeoh, star of *Crouching Tiger, Hidden Dragon;* a wedding dress for Gong Li; and is regularly called upon by a mounting number of idols.

With his roots in Hong Kong, Barney Cheng has lived as far afield as Paris and Canada; and this rich and diverse background has provided an inspirational base for his exclusive and unique collections. Creating new trends in Hong Kong, he uses

unique textures, fabrics and colours to create strong and visually striking designs. His clothes are sensual and tactile with beautiful velvets, hand embroidery and exquisite beading. In his own words, "with such vivid tones and multiple textures, these are not clothes for the shy and retiring".

Having recently opened a bridal suite on Duddell Street in Central, Barney Cheng creates some of most imaginative, stunning and exclusive wedding gowns, bridesmaid dresses and flower girl collections. Beyond fashion, this exclusive salon is a unique one-stop wedding location with a jewellery corner showcasing limited edition creations and a collection of stunning homeware items, all designed by Barney Cheng, along with a full-service bridal salon and wedding registry. Everything within the store evokes a sense of magnificent haute-living, from the Duchesse satin-enveloped fitting room to the hand-beaded sofas. An entourage of knowledgeable advisors are there to guide

you through French laces, Swiss embroideries, Italian Crepes and fine Chinese heavy silks while you enjoy an espresso or green tea.

With an atelier selling Cheng designs exclusively to Lane Crawford in Hong Kong and their increasing number of appearances on the red carpet worldwide, Barney Cheng has become a label that the rich and famous are proud to have hanging in their wardrobe.

FACTS
PRODUCTS	bridal gowns • ladies' wear • homeware • gifts • jewellery • accessories
FEATURES	exclusive designs • custom-made items • full-service bridal salon • wedding registry
NEARBY	Lan Kwai Fong • Hollywood Road • ifc mall • Star Ferry
CONTACT	bridal shop: 1 Duddell Street, Central, Hong Kong • telephone: +852.2905 1011 • facsimile: +852.3011 6248 • email: celebration@barneycheng.com studio: 12/F Worldwide Comm Bldg, 34 Wyndham Street, Central, Hong Kong • telephone: +852.2530 2829 • facsimile: 852.2530 2835 • email: bureau@barneycheng.com • website: www.barneycheng.com

PHOTOGRAPHS COURTESY OF BARNEY CHENG.

Carnet Jewellery

Michelle Ong and Avi Nagar established Carnet Jewellery in 2003 but their dynamic working relationship goes back more than 20 years. In this short time Carnet Jewellery has gained an unrivalled reputation in Asia and has garnered huge international recognition. Indeed, with comparisons to the prominent JAR in Paris, Carnet is already considered by some as one of the most influential present-day jewellery designers.

Designed by world-renowned architect Edward Tuttle, the magnificent Shop 114 in Chater House has been transformed into an exclusive elegant gallery since January

...the designs are bold and artistic yet sophisticated and sensual.

2007 to showcase the gorgeous Carnet creations. Customers who wish to own a piece of luxury are encouraged to visit Carnet's stunning Shop 119 in Prince's Building, which is also a masterpiece of Tuttle. Lush and luxurious, the shop captivates and tempts with its alluring, glittering showpieces.

Fusing creative influences from the East and West, Carnet's collections include one-of-a-kind and signed limited editions. Made with traditional craftsmanship, the designs are bold and artistic yet sophisticated and sensual.

Black lace cuffs studded with diamonds create a sexy finish to a little black dress; brooches dripping in grapes of diamonds and gemstones are great for celebratory occasions; and vibrant emeralds, rubies, sapphires and black diamonds are transformed into elegant watches, sparkling necklaces and exquisite earrings.

Appearing miles from their happy roots in Hong Kong, Carnet designs are sold at Harvey Nichols in London and have been auctioned through Christie's and Sotheby's. Sought after worldwide, Carnet jewels have become regular features along the red carpets of Hollywood and are worn by celebrities such as Jennifer Garner, Glenn Close, Teri Hatcher, Kate Winslet and so on.

Following her reputation as a famous jewellery designer, Michelle Ong was invited to design pieces for the Hollywood blockbuster *The Da Vinci Code* in which, among others, you can see the Fleur de Lys Cross Key—a beautiful pendant of platinum and 18-karat gold—and the Cross—a sultry black diamond pin, set in platinum.

With or without such impressive endorsements, Carnet's definitive success is due to its passion and flair; and, on any shopping trip to Central, it would be sacrilege not to drop by to appreciate this true art and add a sparkle to your eye.

THIS PAGE: Part of the Black Lace collection, these stunning earrings are encrusted with brilliant cut diamonds and expertly mounted on 18-karat white gold.

OPPOSITE: Shop 114 in Chater House has been transformed into an exclusive gallery.

PHOTOGRAPHS COURTESY OF CARNET JEWELLERY.

FACTS

PRODUCTS	hand-crafted jewellery set with diamonds and precious stones • timepieces
FEATURES	stunning showroom • internationally renowned label • one-off designs
NEARBY	Star Ferry • ifc mall • Lan Kwai Fong • Soho
CONTACT	shop: Shop 119, Prince's Building, First Floor, 10 Chater House, Central, Hong Kong • telephone: +852.2805 0113 • facsimile: +852.2805 0180 • email: shop@carnetjewellery.com office: Suite 505, Peter Building, 58 Queen's Road, Central, Hong Kong • telephone: +852.2526 5194 • facsimile: +852.2845 9276 • email: carnet@carnetjewellery.com • website: www.carnetjewellery.com •

Covatta Design

Hong Kong has long been recognised for its wealth of traditional Chinese tailors. For years visitors and residents have been measuring up for everything from custom-made suits to authentic cheongsam dresses. Now, with Hong Kong's increasingly recognised status on the worldwide fashion scene, times are changing and the city is offering some progressively glamorous alternatives to the backstreet tailor.

Covatta Design, specialising in stunning bespoke jewellery and accessories, has become a prevalent name in this sophisticated market and presents an exciting and truly unique extravagance.

Offering the most luxurious of services, designer Mary Covatta meets with every client to build an individual brief based on their character, style and requirements. From a gift for a special occasion to an everyday

necklace, each concept and specific need is carefully considered; and the end result is both dazzling and delightfully customised. Original sketches become fantastic objects—from vibrant beaded necklaces to elegantly carved silver bracelets.

Unlike most ateliers, Covatta Design holds no signature pieces. Each earring, necklace or ring is wonderfully different; one could see, however, a consistency in the quality and craftsmanship that flow through all the designs.

Passionate for vivid colours and uneven shapes of natural stones, many of Mary Covatta's concepts incorporate magnificent gemstones such as turquoise, amber and jade. Mary Covatta's success began when friends asked her to help design individual

THIS PAGE (FROM TOP): Covatta Design offers luxurious services in designing glamorous jewellery for different clients; natural materials are used to create the bracelets.

OPPOSITE (FROM TOP): Each accessory is put together skillfully and creatively; clients can have their jewellery customised according to their character and style.

...specialising in stunning bespoke jewellery and accessories...

pieces for them. Now, as Covatta Design's reputation grows beyond Asia, international clients call upon her creativity and expertise. Locally in Hong Kong, you can still call Mary for a private appointment at your apartment or hotel to dream up sparkling adornments over a cup of tea, or even to go through your wardrobe to think up a complementary ensemble. Whether you're here on a short visit or are a long-term resident, Covatta Design caters to individual requests and

offers a more unique and distinctive alternative to what the more established global brands provide.

With an eye for all things beautiful, Mary Covatta's expertise stretches beyond jewellery design—a range of other services include textiles and interior design. With over 20 years of experience in Australia and Hong Kong, both you and your home could enjoy the satisfactory results of a pair of experienced and wildly creative hands.

FACTS

PRODUCTS custom-made jewellery • accessories • textiles • interior design
FEATURES Unique custom-made products • sophisticated service
CONTACT telephone: +852.3118 7381 • facsimile: +852.2525 5118 • email: design@covatta.net • website: www.covattadesign.com

PHOTOGRAPHS COURTESY OF COVATTA DESIGN.

G.O.D.

THIS PAGE (ANTI-CLOCKWISE FROM TOP):
G.O.D. uses quality fabrics and materials for its furniture; eye-catching store front; creatively decorated showroom.

OPPOSITE (ANTI-CLOCKWISE FROM TOP):
Quirky and fun, G.O.D.'s furniture is distinctive; G.O.D.'s 'Double Happiness' range of products; using eclectic designs, patterns, textures and colours, G.O.D. has captured the imagination of the modern-day consumer.

Whether G.O.D. is an abbreviation of 'Goods of Desire' or the Cantonese slang 'to live better', there is certainly no doubt that this Hong Kong-based chain of funky, fun and fashionable lifestyle products lives up to both analogies. Its colourful and dynamic boutiques and showrooms across the city provide an entertaining and exciting shopping experience for those kitting out their flats or merely browsing for gifts.

With a strong local flavour to their designs, the core range of G.O.D.'s products are conceived in-house using Asia's finest materials and ceramics while the rest are made up of top quality brands such as Dualit, Epicurean and Mobydee. Sumptuous cushions and soft furnishings made of raw silk and linen bring a vivid Oriental spirit to the shop. Chinese lanterns hang alongside retro lampshades, creating a visual treat of eclectic ideas, colours and patterns.

Combining casual style with comfortable living, their furniture range uses unusual materials and quirky edges to bring out G.O.D.'s sense of character and trademark humour—from the giant hands that pose as surprisingly comfortable chairs to the oversized chrome lamp shades.

G.O.D. caters to every aspect of your lifestyle and you will find the store filled with everything from relaxing sofa beds and huge wooden wardrobes to funky aprons and

...funky, fun and fashionable lifestyle products...

With four stores now scattered across Hong Kong, you will find the brand's distinctively unique products available on Hong Kong Island in Central and Causeway Bay; and in Kowloon, at Harbour City in Tsim Sha Tsui. G.O.D. also wholesales to retailers in parts of Asia, USA and Europe. Already considered one of the top ten brands in Hong Kong, G.O.D.'s growing recognition on an international scale has set plans in motion to open individual stores in other countries.

lacquered chopsticks. So if you want something wacky, fun and bold, you will certainly find it in G.O.D.'s carefully laid out sections dedicated to homeware, kitchenware, bathware, lighting, books and stationery. G.O.D. even has a range of clothes; cool, casual items such as vintage 'Double Happiness' T-shirts and tote bags created from stylised photographs depicting nostalgic aspects of life in Hong Kong.

PHOTOGRAPHS COURTESY OF G.O.D.

FACTS

PRODUCTS	lifestyle • furniture • kitchenware • bed linen • bathware • clothes • stationery
FEATURES	wacky designs • huge selection • in-house designers
NEARBY	Causeway Bay
CONTACT	Leighton Centre, Sharp Street East, Causeway Bay • tel: +852.2890 5555 • 48, Hollywood Road, Central • tel: +852.2805 1876 • 3/F Hong Kong Hotel, Harbour City, Tsim Sha Tsui, Kowloon • tel: +852.2784 5555 • email: info@god.com.hk • website: www.god.com.hk

Kou

Interior designer extraordinaire Lu Kou has created a stunning concept with her lifestyle boutique, Kou. Styled in a luxury penthouse with staggering views out to Victoria Harbour, Kou is a showpiece home of pure epicurean indulgence. Keeping up with Hong Kong's thirst for glamour, Lu Kou has provided a sensational shopping experience displaying designer lifestyle products throughout the apartment. Looking like it might belong to one of Hong Kong's rich and famous, this is one of few apartments you'll be rewarded for rummaging through the kitchen drawers and bathroom cabinets. All that you see, minus the view, is for sale. As you browse, you'll come across everything from sexy lingerie by Tina Barrett to outdoor furniture by Kettal.

The lift doors open straight into a magnificent lounge area, which in turn opens up onto a lush outdoor terrace. Rich purple walls are covered in a selection of

...a showpiece home of pure epicurean indulgence.

artwork by both local and international artists; Persian rugs from Isfahan and Beluchi tribes are thrown across the stone floor; gigantic suede sofas gather around the fireplace; and, covering every available surface are exquisite ornaments, vases, sculptures and lamps. In the kitchen, crystal glassware—hand-picked from Belgium—stands elegantly on the work surface while laid out in the drawers are cutlery from Thiers in France. Downstairs, a library and study are filled with more rugs, an armchair and shelves stacked with books. The grand master bedroom is dominated by a stately double bed, lavished in indulgent linens and silks and surrounded by fragrant candles from Vie Luxe. Next door in the dressing room, Oriental lounge wear designed by Lu Kou hangs alongside other designer labels while lingerie by Chantal Thomass is folded neatly in the drawers. The en-suite bathroom is appropriately used to exhibit beautiful-smelling bath and beauty products.

Walking through the apartment, with a glass of bubbling vintage Krug in hand, the atmosphere is decidedly opulent, mixing ornate traces of 19th-century Europe with the fresh simplicity of Southeast Asian design. An antique chandelier hangs high above a sleek modern sofa while an elaborate heavy table, already set for a banquet, is concealed behind a delicate Oriental screen. With items from Bali, Thailand, China and Europe spanning across centuries right up to the modern day, Kou is a lavish and eclectic gallery of all things luxurious that will keep you popping back for more.

FACTS

PRODUCTS	designer lifestyle products • fashion and accessories • bath and beauty products • interior consultancy • home accessorising
FEATURES	stunning apartment to showcase products • champagne • ladies lunches • wine seminars • cigar evenings
NEARBY	Central • ifc mall • Star Ferry
CONTACT	Kou, 22F Fung House, 19-20 Connaught Road, Central, Hong Kong • telephone: +852.2530 2234 • facsimile: +852.2849 4771 • email: info@kouconcept.com • website: www.kouconcept.com

PHOTOGRAPHS COURTESY OF KOU.

Lane Crawford IFC Mall

THIS PAGE (CLOCKWISE FROM TOP):
Beautiful art installation gives a
refined touch to the store;
a chic and tasteful CD bar;
sit in the lap of luxury at the
Platinum Suite.

OPPOSITE (FROM LEFT): Shoppers
quench their thirst at the
glamourously cool Martini Bar;
designer homeware and
furniture pieces on display.

With a history of over 150 years in Hong Kong, Lane Crawford is a longstanding hallmark of the city's thriving retail scene. It has four distinct stores, the flagship being at the International Finance Centre, the ifc mall. It has dedicated the 7,618 sq m (82,000 sq ft) flagship store to absolute luxury and offers a unique shopping experience.

The store is creatively distributed into gallery-like spaces to house fashion within different environments.

With the largest range of international designers and contemporary brands encompassing departments for fashion, lingerie, cosmetics, shoes and accessories, fine jewellery, home and lifestyle, you will find everything you need.

This flagship store combines fashion with art and architecture. Internationally renowned designers George Yabu and Glenn Pushelberg were commissioned to create the store's interiors. The store is stunning and

...Lane Crawford redefines the art of pampering in shopping.

dramatic, creating the ultimate platform on which to showcase Lane Crawford's exquisite collections. Golden mosaics, beautiful custom-made wallpapers and dazzling ceilings set a luxurious backdrop for the designer collections.

The service at this store rivals that of a five-star hotel, with a concierge to welcome you, personal stylists to navigate you through the gallery-like rooms and a cosmetic concierge to offer advice and beauty tips. With styling and makeovers, complimentary home delivery and an

ordering service for flowers, cakes and chocolates, Lane Crawford redefines the art of pampering in shopping.

For the exclusive Platinum Card holders, a platinum service is available offering an array of specialised events and VIP services. The terrace restaurant includes views directly across the Harbour and the red-lacquered Martini Bar adds a little glamour for everyday shoppers. And while you recharge at the Martini Bar, you can also recharge your phone battery and take advantage of the free web access to check your email.

With every shopper's whim and fancy catered to and a lavish store in which to shop, Lane Crawford ifc mall is indeed the place for the ultimate shopping experience.

FACTS

PRODUCTS men's and women's fashion • beauty • shoes and accessories • fine jewellery • home and lifestyle

FEATURES personal stylists • cosmetic concierge • complimentary home delivery • terrace restaurant • martini bar

NEARBY ifc mall • Central • Star Ferry

CONTACT Lane Crawford, Podium 3, ifc mall, 8 Finance Street, Central, Hong Kong • telephone: +852.2118 3388 • facsimile: +852.2118 3389 • email: customerrelationship@lanecrawford.com • website: www.lanecrawford.com

PHOTOGRAPHS COURTESY OF LANE CRAWFORD.

Lane Crawford Pacific Place

THIS PAGE (FROM TOP): *A sleek and stylish display of home and lifestyle products; the cool, minimalist setting of the men's grooming section.*

OPPOSITE (FROM LEFT): *The spatial design is funky and trendy; the sharp and sleek interiors of the men's fashion department.*

Since 1850, Lane Crawford has gained an unrivalled knowledge base and experience to become a powerful brand in Hong Kong's commercial environment.

With four stores located across Hong Kong, Lane Crawford has created different environments in each store that focus on a different target market.

In Pacific Place, within the modern architecture of chrome and glass, Lane Crawford has immersed itself in hi-tech and hi-design, using highly innovative and state-of-the-art interactive technology to provide a whole new unique shopping experience that appeals to young fashionable trendsetters.

Opening up a market for a new generation of designers and contemporary collections, together with internationally renowned fashion brands, the selection here is sharp and modern. Lane Crawford at Pacific Place is Hong Kong's premier destination for stylish collections by up-and-coming fashion designers. The dominant theme for its interior design is modern and progressive with hi-tech features: interactive screens that morph as shoppers walk past; sales counters created with a heat-sensitive finish that responds to touch by changing colour.

There is a CD Bar installed with i-Pod stations where they play the latest music and where DJs host live sessions on weekends. There is even an 'i-bar' where you can check your e-mail, browse through magazines and be entertained by host of in-store services. It is the perfect place for guys or girls to hang out and

shop through 4,645 sq m (50,000 sq ft) of fashion, shoes, bags, jewellery, cosmetics, home and lifestyle.

Stunning graphics continue throughout the store with custom-made wallpapers, dramatic mirrors and silk-screens, all used to vivid effect in colours ranging from dusky charcoal to luminous pink and yellow. Lane Crawford has yet again reinforced its status as one of Hong Kong's leading fashion destinations.

FACTS

PRODUCTS	men's and women's fashion • beauty • shoes and accessories • fine jewellery • home and lifestyle
FEATURES	CD bar • Internet access
NEARBY	Pacific Place Mall • Admiralty • Wan Chai
CONTACT	Lane Crawford, Pacific Place, 88 Queensway, Admiralty, Hong Kong • telephone: +852.2118 3668 • facsimile: +852.2118 3669 • email: customerrelationship@lanecrawford.com • website: www.lanecrawford.com

PHOTOGRAPHS COURTESY OF LANE CRAWFORD.

Lane Crawford Times Square

Promoting a diverse range of international designers and contemporary labels, Burberry Diane von Furstenberg, Canali, Boss Hugo Boss, Vanessa Bruno, and premium denim brands such as Superfine and Rag & Bone. Lane Crawford is Hong Kong's ultimate fashion store. With world-renowned labels filling the racks and prominent local designers such as Dorian Ho displaying their exquisite collections, it offers the largest assortment of casual and couture fashion and apparel. With the Asian market quickly developing, Lane Crawford has expanded to mainland China and it has gained a reputation as one of the leading luxury retailers in Greater China.

Firmly established in Hong Kong since 1850, Lane Crawford has four stores across the city, each with a unique

THIS PAGE (FROM TOP): A section ladies can't do without—the shoe collection; the dominant store at Times Square, Lane Crawford impresses with high, ornate ceilings and marble floors.

OPPOSITE (FROM LEFT): High-end designer menswear; a beauty hall filled with cosmetics from luxury brands.

personality. Fusing fashion and art, the design in each store is distinct and dramatic; people go to admire the architecture as much the designer collections on display. Their oldest store, in Times Square, Causeway Bay, is now a distinguished landmark in Hong Kong. Times Square is the city's centre to meet, celebrate and shop. With its famed clock tower and gigantic video screens, people congregate around the square to count down festivals, watch live entertainment and of course experience some of the city's best shopping. Strategically placed in the mall, Lane Crawford is without doubt the most popular attraction, offering an impressive and exciting environment to shop in and the most diverse range of fashion labels and brands.

There has been a recent expansion of their cosmetics area. Now, Lane Crawford has the largest selection of exclusive beauty products including lines from world-renowned brands such as La Mer, Laura Mercier, Bliss, and Skinn for men.

As Hong Kong's urban sprawl continues skywards, more and more shopping malls are opening across the city. Causeway Bay still remains the city's busiest shopping district, but Lane Crawford has little competition when it comes to its phenomenal collection of designer labels.

PHOTOGRAPHS COURTESY OF LANE CRAWFORD.

FACTS

PRODUCTS	men's and women's fashion • beauty • shoes and accessories • fine jewellery • home and lifestyle
FEATURES	personal styling • makeovers • home delivery
NEARBY	Times Square • Causeway Bay • Happy Valley • Victoria Park
CONTACT	Lane Crawford, Times Square, 1 Matheson Street, Causeway Bay, Hong Kong • telephone: +852.2118 3638 • facsimile: +852.2118 3588 • email: customerrelationship@lanecrawford.com • website: www.lanecrawford.com

OVO

In a stunning showroom located deep in the heart of Hong Kong's bustling Wan Chai district, OVO, Hong Kong's leading lifestyle store, displays its uniquely stylised furniture with a wonderful, eclectic mix of homeware accessories. Filling the shelves, the tables and walls, you'll find everything from flamboyant cushion covers to earthy lamps, giant wooden sculptures to abstract glass vases, as well as an impressive display of original artwork. Covering 930 sq m (10, 000 sq ft), temptations are abundant; and the serene, sophisticated atmosphere merely adds to the excitement of there being so many beautiful things on offer.

Created in 2000 by a group of award-winning designers, OVO (the name is drawn from the company's motto, 'Original and Vivid with a touch of Oriental beauty') initially dedicated its brand name to their in-house designed furniture, which is now considered some of the best in the city. With a flair for refined, understated design, their modern concepts are still inspired and influenced by

THIS PAGE: Superbly styled, OVO's vast showroom is a great solution for those in need of some lifestyle inspiration.

OPPOSITE: Placing all the goods into a context, shoppers are able to conceive how the pieces will work in their own home.

a touch of Asian style and, as a result, OVO furniture is recognised for its sleek, simplistic design and exceptional quality.

Aligning itself with nature, there is a prominent use of natural materials such as stone, oak and cowhide. Each stunning piece is available in varying fabrics and can be custom-made to suit your requirements. They include elegant L-shaped sofas, four-part tables that can be used independently or sculpted together, Chinese-style dining chairs and beautiful leather armchairs.

Regularly updating their designs OVO has a growing number of products including their recent esZENtials line which, as the name suggests, is formed around the notion of peace and harmony in the home. The luxurious chairs and unique, Asian-inspired coffee tables would certainly receive approval from any feng shui expert.

Now, alongside the success of their stylish furniture, the store encompasses a range of lifestyle goods, making OVO a

reliable source for providing anything your home may lack. You can find bedlinen, lighting, kitchenware, sculptures, paintings, CDs, books and spa products.

OVO Garden is dedicated to flowers, plants and spectacular vases. Using their expertise, you can be sure everything in

OVO is beautifully designed and guaranteed to be of the best quality. And with a professional consultancy service to provide advice on the use of colour and space in your home, you have the opportunity to create your very own oasis that will be as eye-catching as their Wan Chai showroom.

FACTS

PRODUCTS	in-house designed furniture • lifestyle products
FEATURES	custom designs available • professional consultancy • exceptional quality • marriage of East and West
NEARBY	Wan Chai • Star Street • Pacific Place
CONTACT	OVO Home, GF 16 Queen's Road East, Wan Chai, Hong Kong • telephone: +852.2526 7226 • facsimile: +852.2526 7227 • email: info@ovo.com.hk • website: www.ovo.com.hk OVO Garden, GF 16 Wing Fung Street, Wan Chai, Hong Kong telephone: +852.2529 2599 • facsimile: +852.2529 2569 • email: info@ovogarden.com.hk • website: www.ovogarden.com.hk

PHOTOGRAPHS COURTESY OF OVO.

Pacific Place

Fifteen years ago, Pacific Place opened as the largest and most dynamic real estate project that Hong Kong had ever witnessed. Today, this pioneer in the competitive retail industry is still leading the pack. In fact, Pacific Place is the comprehensive complex that redefined the geographical boundaries of Hong Kong Island's Central district. With its prime location, superb design and advanced technology, it remains as Hong Kong's premier destination for luxury shopping, entertainment, dining, working, conferencing and accommodation all under one roof. The complex occupies over 510,000 sq m (5.5 million sq ft) in total.

...Hong Kong's premier destination for luxury shopping, entertainment, dining, working...

Incorporating three five-star hotels, over 140 shops, stylish restaurants, major departmental stores, luxury serviced apartments, three prestigious office towers and a well-equipped conference centre, Pacific Place is truly a highly self-sufficient, integrated complex.

All seamlessly connected, guests from the JW Marriott Hotel, the Conrad and Island Shangri-La can enjoy direct access to the impressive 65,000 sq m (700,000 sq ft) of luxury shopping whilst having unobstructed access to Admiralty Mass Transit Railway (MTR), the major interchange station on Hong Kong Island. With only one stop away from the Airport Express Line by MTR or 5 minutes by taxi, within walking distance to the Star Ferry and the Peak Tram, and a stone's throw from other tourist spots such as Golden Bauhinia Square, Hong Kong Convention and Exhibition Centre and Hong Kong Park, its location is unprecedented. In fact, Pacific Place itself makes the area a prime destination for tourists and residents. The recently emerging bars, restaurants, boutiques and galleries along the adjoining Starstreet precinct are further enticements that draw visitors to this lively neighbourhood.

Spreading over four floors and with over 140 fashion brands and restaurants, Pacific Place Mall has an impressive

collection of department stores and boutiques carrying merchandise and apparel from well-known international brands and designer labels. White marble walkways, glass roofs, open elevators and sleek galleria levels create an elegant shopping environment. With everything from fashion to flowers, from AV gadgets to personal accessories, and from costume jewellery to custom jewellery, one's entire shopping list can be catered to in here. Furthermore, deemed as one of the poshest malls in Hong Kong, Pacific Place remains the most sought-after destination for luxury boutiques. Indeed, it is the only mall in Hong Kong to house two elite department stores, making it a convenient base for high-end shopping.

Lane Crawford has recently renovated its store here with a unique and creative store design. Displaying the most extensive range of designer fashion along with a lifestyle and cosmetics department, you can find all things luxurious and lavish within the ultra-modern and vibrant atmosphere. Seibu has its flagship store in Pacific Place. This is the destination for contemporary fashion and accessories, with creative designer labels and cool casual wear.

Many upmarket international and local labels have also opened standalone stores in the mall. Prestigious and exclusive

...Pacific Place remains the most sought-after destination for luxury boutiques.

THIS PAGE (FROM TOP): *Pacific Place is the place to buy the latest season of clothes from high-fashion labels; the complex is an excellent venue for inspirational events.*

OPPOSITE: *There will be no shortage of choice when it comes to culinary delights at Pacific Place.*

brands include Burberry, Celine, Chanel, Chloé, Dior, Fendi, Gucci, Lanvin, Loewe and Prada sit alongside reputable stores such as agnès b., D&G Dolce & Gabbana, Emporio Armani, Just Cavalli, Hugo Boss, Joyce, Marc by Marc Jacobs, Swank and Vivienne Tam. For the latest designer accessories, check out Bottega Veneta, Hermes, Louis Vuitton, Manolo Blahnik or Salvatore Ferragamo.

For something a little sparklier, visit the Watch and Jewellery Gallery. Here you can find the world's finest jewels and watches under the world acclaimed brands such as Bvlgari, Cartier, Jaeger-LeCoultre, Piaget, Roger Dubuis, Tiffany & Co. and Van Cleef & Arpels.

Hong Kong's top-notch lifestyle supermarket, Great Food Hall, is also housed within the giant complex. Not limited to just fashion and accessories, Pacific Place is a great location for anyone in search of music, AV equipment and electronics too. With renowned brands such as Bang & Olufsen selling the latest in designer gadgets and home entertainment systems, as well as other audio and video centres offering valuable advice, rest assured that only the best quality products are on selection. Hong Kong Records is a must-visit if you want to stock up on the latest CDs and DVDs.

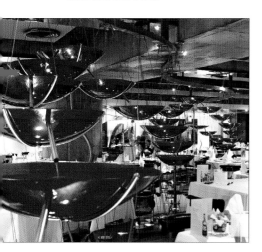

Setting Pacific Place apart from other malls is an established prominence of local interest stores. Among brands with a strong cultural overtone and top designer labels such as Shanghai Tang, visitors can find exquisite Chinese boutiques selling beautiful gift items, from antique knick-knacks to chic fashion and homeware. Chinese Arts and Crafts is filled with collectibles, Chinese handicrafts and ancient treasures; while Liu Li Gong Fang stocks modern glass art pieces.

Those who love food but are in a hurry will be delighted by Pacific Place's magnificent Foodfare. Solar-glass panels create the impression of an al fresco dining hall. For the food gourmets, over 20 dining outlets in the mall and in the three hotels serve up scrumptious dishes. With such a generous selection of food, it is the place to enjoy whichever type of cuisine you fancy. Light, zesty lunches, delicious pastries and authentic fine dining from Italian, Japanese, Chinese and

Western restaurants and bars are all conveniently located in elegant, stylish settings. Relax and sip a soothing cup of coffee in Cova's casual al fresco ambience; enjoy mouth-watering pizzas and pasta at the recently renovated Grappa's; and dine with nightly live music at yè shanghai—you will be spoilt for choice when it comes to picking your favourite gastronomic delight. Besides the diverse range of eating places in Pacific Place, visitors can also choose from the fine restaurants and bars within the three hotels. This means an even greater choice in exquisite culinary experiences such as the breezy Fish Bar with its harbour view at the JW Marriott Hotel, the delectable Cantonese cuisine at the Conrad's Golden Leaf, and the award-winning Restaurant Petrus that serves contemporary French food at the Island Shangri-La.

Providing the ultimate shopping experience with a glamorous collection of department stores and boutiques as well as enticing, contemporary restaurants, Pacific Place also lends itself to a variety of entertainment activities, regularly hosting

inspirational events from fashion shows and design exhibitions to musical and charity galas such as "A Love Affair with Shoes" and "Music Lives—A Tribute to Mozart". There is also a multi-screen, stadium seating cinema complex offering the latest blockbusters. Collectively, Pacific Place is a unique, integrated complex that has successfully established itself as a centre for world-class business and pleasure.

THIS PAGE (FROM TOP): *Offering a diverse range of high-end merchandise and apparel, up-market department stores and standalone boutiques can all be found at Pacific Place.*

OPPOSITE: *Four floors of superb shopping and great buys.*

PHOTOGRAPHS COURTESY OF PACIFIC PLACE.

FACTS

PRODUCTS	high fashion • accessories • lifestyle • fine dining • hotels • serviced apartments
FEATURES	luxurious shopping environment • 3 five-star hotels • 3 grade-A office towers • 1 conference centre
NEARBY	Starstreet precinct • Star Ferry • The Peak Tram • Central • Golden Bauhinia Square • Hong Kong Park
CONTACT	Pacific Place, 88 Queensway, Hong Kong • telephone: +852.2844 8988 • email: ppshopping@swireproperties.com • website: www.pacificplace.com.hk

Schoeni Art Gallery

Opened in 1992, Schoeni Art Gallery was the love child of the late Manfred Schoeni, whose dedication and passion to the arts forged an unprecedented relationship with China by bringing numerous artists into the international limelight. The gallery has since played a pivotal role in building the importance and global recognition of China as a serious player in the art world; and, as a result, many collectors are turning their heads eastwards. Having hosted over 150 exhibitions in their Hong Kong gallery and organised hundreds more around the world, Schoeni Art Gallery has an unrivalled knowledge in Chinese contemporary art.

The gallery is professionally recognised around the world as an established platform from which highly talented and previously unknown contemporary artists have launched themselves into the art scene. Artists such as Yue Min Jun, Yang Shao Bin,

...the gallery is devotedly moving forward in the discovery of Chinese contemporary art.

Wang Yi Dong, Li Gui Jun and Zhang Lin Hai have all celebrated their first overseas exhibitions at Schoeni Art Gallery.

The gallery is now managed by Manfred's daughter, Nicole Schoeni. Inheriting his vision and drive, Nicole ensures that Schoeni Art Gallery continues to discover China's best, fresh talents; and is pushing Chinese art more than ever into the mainstream. Working alongside Shanghai Tang for their limited edition Spring 2006 collection, Nicole has brought contemporary art and fashion together and is drawing attention from both critics and designers alike.

Not ending with fashion, Schoeni Art Gallery's expertise has also been used by the Grand Hyatt, who sought advice for their most prestigious hotel in the renowned Jin Mao Tower in Shanghai. In a similar form, exclusive members bars, The China Club in Hong Kong and The China Club in Berlin have asked for guidance regarding their significant collections of antiques and art.

In Hong Kong you can view Schoeni's collection of over 2,000 paintings and spanning over 100 artists, in two galleries on Old Bailey Street and Hollywood Road. Regular events and exhibitions promote both established and emerging Chinese artists; the gallery is devotedly moving forward in the discovery of Chinese contemporary art.

The sister company, Wai Yin and Dave, has specialised in the traditional restoration of stunning Chinese antique furniture for over 15 years; and is close by on Chancery Lane with a further showroom in Aberdeen and a huge warehouse in Zhongshan, Mainland China. The Schoeni Family has a strong foothold in China's past and future.

FACTS

PRODUCTS	Chinese contemporary art
FEATURES	established and emerging Chinese artists • vast collection • regular events
NEARBY	Central
CONTACT	Schoeni Art Gallery, 21–31 Old Bailey Street, Central, Hong Kong • Branch Gallery, 27 Hollywood Road, Central, Hong Kong • telephone: +852.2869 8802 • fascimile: +852.2522 1528 • email: gallery@schoeni.com.hk • website: www.schoeni.com.hk

PHOTOGRAPHS COURTESY OF SCHOENI ART GALLERY.

Shanghai Tang

Using bold designs, luxurious materials and brilliant colours, Shanghai Tang has created a distinctive style that is recognised and admired around the world. Opened in 1994 as a small tailoring boutique in Hong Kong, China's world-class luxury brand now operates outlets in the fashion capitals of London, Paris, New York and Tokyo as well as branches in Shanghai—the origin of its inspiration.

At its inception, Shanghai Tang offered a made-to-measure clothing service that clearly followed in the footsteps of the Shanghainese tailors of the 1930s. As the Cultural Revolution dampened the thirst for inventive fashion and the ancient art of qi pao making (with its painstaking attention to detail and craftsmanship) dwindled, tailors turned their concentration to men's suits. Today, employing the few specialists who remain, Shanghai Tang keeps the qi pao in fashion, radically redesigning the snug-fitting dress to new heights of elegance.

Finding inspiration for all its clothes, homeware and accessory designs in Chinese culture, Shanghai Tang has teamed up with Hong Kong's Schoeni Art Gallery for its latest collection 'Chuang Yi' themed on Chinese contemporary art. Schoeni Art Gallery has introduced some of the country's most eminent artists to the international arena and has collaborated

THIS PAGE (FROM LEFT): Modern Chinese details are juxtaposed against traditional Chinese décor at the flagship store in the historic Pedder Building; the collaboration with world-respected Schoeni Art Gallery created a unique and stylish limited collection of products.

OPPOSITE (FROM LEFT): The peony coat from a summer range; vivid colours, a trademark of Shanghai Tang, influence the style of homeware goods.

...uniquely cut; brilliantly different with an instantly recognisable quality.

approach to fashion. Using exquisite silks, velvets, cashmeres and linens alongside their trademark vibrant colours, each design is uniquely cut; brilliantly different with an instantly recognisable quality.

Famous for their elegant Chinese-style jackets and beautiful clothing line, Shanghai Tang also designs children's wear, toys and accessories. In addition, a homeware series is available for those who wish to stamp their homes with Shanghai Tang's exceptional sense of style and quirkiness.

Its Hong Kong flagship store is deemed by many as one of the most prestigious boutiques around. Its sense of extravagance and opulence sweeps the two floors. The sumptuous décor includes a dark wooden floor, Chinese art, bespoke wallpapers and vivid collections, all making for a stunning gallery. With smaller stores located in Pacific Place, The Peninsula Hotel, The InterContinental Hotel

with Shanghai Tang to issue a limited edition collection that includes a satin bag, a velvet Tang jacket, leather-bound photo album and porcelain plate created and signed by five important Chinese artists.

With collections changing every season, Shanghai Tang consistently designs with a dynamic and fearless

and another two at the airport, very few visitors to Hong Kong will escape the lure of Shanghai Tang—it would be a real shame if they did.

FACTS

PRODUCTS	clothing • homeware • accessories
FEATURES	beautiful shop design • custom-design clothing • dynamic and vibrant design
NEARBY	central • ifc mall • Star Ferry
CONTACT	Shanghai Tang, Pedder Building, 12 Pedder Street, Central, Hong Kong • telephone: +852.2537 2888 • facsimile: +852.2156 9898 • email: contactus@shanghaitang.com • website: www.shanghaitang.com

PHOTOGRAPHS COURTESY OF SHANGHAI TANG.

Sonjia

With its vibrant street markets and luxurious designer boutiques, Hong Kong attracts people from across the world who eagerly arrive to lose themselves among the bustling lanes of its multiple shopping districts. Within the city, a cosmopolitan and highly fashionable society have clicked their designer heels along these shop-lined streets, and opened the way for a growing number of designers to create their diverse, often flamboyant, collections. Hong Kong is at last reaching the forefront of world fashion, and it's doing so in dazzling style. Standing out with her spectacular and dramatic ideas, Sonjia Norman, while based in Hong Kong, is gaining international recognition for her individualistic and fun designs. Her original showroom is a must-visit on your shopping itinerary in Hong Kong.

Her boutique and design studio is located down a narrow lane close to the lively and hip Star Street. The showroom has a distressed, industrial feel with everything stripped back to reveal its original shell. Stones walls and a concrete floor are fitted with exposed wood, and rusted steel used to

THIS PAGE (FROM TOP): The boutique has a raw and industrial feel; Sonjia Norman uses leather, fur and other exotic textures to design her garments.
OPPOSITE (FROM LEFT): The Sonjia label boasts edgy, one-off creations that are a cut above the rest.

Sonjia Norman...is gaining international recognition for her individualistic and fun designs.

display the textured, colourful designs. Spread over two levels, the loft area upstairs is used as a production and design area while downstairs, the showroom is used to present her two labels—Sonjia and Chibi.

The location and its striking interior is representative of the designs themselves, which are original, cutting-edge, one-of-a-kind creations that effectively combine rock chic with eco chic. The Sonjia label, found on the back of many of Hong Kong's trendy celebrities, uses leather, fur, suede and sumptuous, textured materials to create stunning layers on garments that vary from distressed leather trenchcoats to fabulous hand-painted jackets. Chibi, originally inspired by yoga, is a range of leisure wear worn by Hollywood celebrities such as Gwyneth Paltrow and Angelina Jolie. Alongside her own designs Sonjia Norman sells selected brands such as Henry Duarte's motorcycle bags from Los Angeles and skin belts from Divine Tribe. Hanging from the branches of a bonsai garden are stunning jewellery selected from around the world.

Clients, visiting by appointment only, can enjoy a laid-back atmosphere, listen to music and drink wine with the host, who treats her showroom as a hangout for friends and visitors as much as a place to inspire her.

FACTS

PRODUCTS	fashion • yoga wear • accessories • selected brands
FEATURES	original showroom • one-off pieces • top-quality service
NEARBY	Wan Chai • Star Street
CONTACT	2 Sun Street, Wan Chai • telephone: +852.2529 6223 • facsimile: +852.2529 6328 • email: info@sonjiaonline.com • website: www.sonjiaonline.com

PHOTOGRAPHS COURTESY OF SONJIA.

Starstreet

If you still associate Hong Kong's dining areas with the image of bustling neon lights and lines of busy restaurants and bars, then it's time you experience something different and more stylish.

Starstreet precinct in Wan Chai—a few well-landscaped streets around Star Street and Three Pacific Place office tower—has been quietly transformed from a serene residential community into a cosy community of restaurants and lifestyle stores. Much like the famed Covent Garden in London and the Latin Quarter in Paris, the Starstreet precinct is the result of a group of visionary entrepreneurs who want to set themselves apart from the mainstream in style. They have chosen a non-conventional location that has not been overwhelmed by the city's bustling pace. With a strong belief in their own concept and a high value attached to exclusivity, what used to be the location for an electrical plant in 1889 is now one of Hong Kong's few creative lifestyle communities lined with art galleries, chic home design outlets, florists, cafés, tea bar, bistros and restaurants. The area also serves

THIS PAGE (BELOW): Starstreet is now an upmarket area with elegant restaurants, cool bars and designer lifestyle stores.

OPPOSITE (FROM LEFT): OVO GARDEN houses beautiful plants and bouquets; OVO home offers stunning custom-made furniture; delectable pizza on demand by Pizza Express.

both local and expatriate communities working at Three Pacific Place and other office buildings, as well as residents in the neighbouring premium residential homes. As a result, Starstreet has become an increasingly lively and quirky place for business lunches, after-work drinks, an escape over a coffee or tea, fashionable dining, and shopping for homeware or art.

Its location plays a vital role in its continuing popularity. Within close proximity to three five-star hotels, seviced apartments and a luxury mall in Pacific Place—Hong Kong's pre-eminent lifestyle destination, Starstreets fits snugly into the new urban Hong Kong. It helps that other major streets around Pacific Place such as Queen's Road East, Wing Fung Street and St Francis Street help contribute to the buzz of the area. Besides a posh destination for lifestyle relaxation, Wan Chai is also the place where culture comes alive in its famous adjoining landmarks such as the Hong Kong Convention and Exhibition Centre, Hong Kong Arts Centre and the Hong Kong Academy for Performing Arts. Having the Star Ferry nearby and a direct link to Admiralty MTR station to be opened in 2007 also means that visitors from Kowloon can enjoy easy access to this area.

An eclectic line-up of trendy boutiques, avant-garde galleries and designer lifestyle stores are scattered around the lanes along Starstreet. OVO's theatrical concept store, OVO home, is filled with custom-made furniture of the highest quality. With sleek sofas, innovative lighting and cool furnishings, their trademark sophisticated designs have become a favourite in Hong Kong. Just across the street, OVO GARDEN's tranquil interior houses beautiful bouquets and tropical plants in simple yet surprisingly delightful ways. At

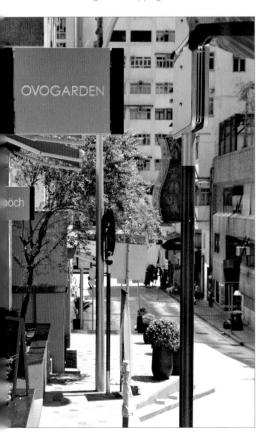

Joineur Family Store, original contemporary designer furniture is made using traditional Chinese wood joinery techniques and hand-crafted by master craftsmen. Agnès b. has opened its first art gallery outside of Paris on Starstreet, once again affirming the area's position as a creative hub. With international photography exhibitions, local art promotions

and a unique bookshop, the agnès b.'s Librairie Galérie adds further diversity and international acclaim to the area. Starstreet also offers local merchandise to those who seek something different and nostalgic. Gitone Fine Arts, an art and ceramics gallery by day, becomes an artistic lifestyle kitchen in the evening, serving up a 12-course authentic Cantonese feast.

Besides shopping, Starstreet is also famous for having some of the city's hippest places to eat and drink.

With sandwich delis, quaint cafés, contemporary teahouses and haute cuisine served up in chic settings, an enticing variety of Eastern and Western hangouts awaits. At one fifth grill, prime-cut steaks and fresh seafood sizzle in the open kitchen while you slink into the deep, plush booths enjoying wine. Right above it, 1/5 one|fifth ultralounge has a fantastic music scene that hosts international DJ acts regularly. Nicely tucked away private rooms also make a sophisticated setting to enjoy their creative list of cocktails. Named after a famous movie studio, Cinecittà is Hong Kong's most stylish Roman Italian restaurant. As fresh and tantalising as its mouth-watering menu, it impresses customers with a glass-encased wine cellar, leather booths and an iconic bar. With a glass shopfront and bistro setting, Pizza Express has established itself in the area for its delectable pizzas and semi-open patio.

Another exceptional restaurant in Starstreet's tempting selection is Ingredients. Essentially French, with influences of Asian and Middle Eastern cuisines, all dishes are freshly prepared for a constantly changing menu. On Wing Fung Street off Star Street, ēpōch illy bar is a clever fusion of illy coffee

tasting and Kosmic Soul music retailing. Customers can consult the DJ there and choose their own music to listen to, be updated on the music scene by the latest magazines and browse through the latest CDs on sale while they relax with a speciality coffee or healthy lunch. There is also a strong representation of Chinese cuisine, all presented in chic and delicate manners. Ming Cha's hip tea bar and salon enables tea lovers to celebrate a renowned selection of rare and distinguished Chinese teas in the most inspiring settings. Xi Yan Sweets presents the best Chinese Southeast Asian treats from Xi Yan's elaborate private kitchen menu in its eye-catching red split-level restaurant.

With such a diverse offering of chic bars, fine restaurants and stylish boutiques, the dynamic area around Starstreet is growing rapidly with more designers and restaurant owners searching out space in the lanes. Already establishing itself as a creative community for Hong Kong's upmarket crowd,

it will not be long before Starstreet becomes synonymous with the city's reputation for sophistication and creativity. Together with exhibitions of inspirational art by distinguished artists from around the world at Three Pacific Place from time to time, Starstreet offers a uniquely pleasant experience that no other precinct can deliver.

THIS PAGE: Xi Yan Sweets is the place to indulge in sweet treats.

OPPOSITE (ANTI-CLOCKWISE FROM TOP): ēpōch illy bar brings the best coffee and music together; the sexy 1/5 one1fifth ultralounge is the ideal place to chill out in; tea lovers love hanging out at Ming Cha for its rare selection of tea.

FACTS
PRODUCTS shopping and entertainment hub • art and cultural events
FEATURES lifestyle boutiques • art galleries • cafés • bars and restaurants
NEARBY Pacific Place • Wan Chai • Central • Wan Chai Star Ferry • Peak Tram • Golden Bauhinia Square • Hong Kong Convention and Exhibition Centre
CONTACT Starstreet, Wan Chai, Hong Kong • email: info@starstreet.com.hk • website: www.starstreet.com.hk

PHOTOGRAPHS COURTESY OF SWIRE PROPERTIES.

Tayma Fine Jewellery

Situated in the prestigious Prince's Building, alongside some of the world's leading high-end brands including Ralph Lauren, Hugo Boss and Chanel, Tayma Fine Jewellery's impressive location is a testament to its superior quality and designs.

One of very few independent boutique brand jewellers in Hong Kong, British designer Tayma Page Allies has acquired an enviable reputation for specialising in rare gemstones for connoisseurs. After 15 years of designing exquisite jewels for Hong Kong's discerning and fashionable crowd, she has built up a loyal following. The boutique-style showroom, decorated with antique French mirrors, cream walls, wooden flooring and luxurious sofas, has a decadent boudoir feel and sets a glamorous backdrop while you search for a new best friend which, in this case, is certainly not limited to diamonds.

Tayma's distinctive and elegant jewels are individually designed for each carefully collected, rare and beautiful-coloured

THIS PAGE (CLOCKWISE FROM TOP):
Shoppers are encouraged to relax as they browse and select their special piece; gemstones for connoisseurs, such as rubellite, are set in diamonds on gold or platinum; antique French mirrors set the tone of the boudoir décor.

OPPOSITE: The elegant exterior gives passers-by a full view of the kind of jewellery they will find inside.

...impressive location is a testament to its superior quality and designs.

TAYMA FINE JEWELLERY

gemstone, accented in fine diamonds and hand-made in gold or platinum. Stunning tear-drop earrings, eye-catching cross pendants, elaborate multi-gemmed bracelets and dazzling cocktail rings make up a sparkling collection of ready-to-wear jewellery. Each piece is hand-made by a team of expert craftsmen and is guaranteed to be a one-off design. The meticulous care invested is evident in the immaculately finished products, and a single piece of jewellery can involve over 500 hours of work.

Tayma Fine Jewellery will also design custom-made jewellery and source the world for specific gemstones and diamonds. Listening to your needs and looking at your lifestyle and personality, Tayma will advise on the perfect gemstones to suit your character and personal style. This kind of attention is reassuring—whether you're searching for a once-in-a-lifetime piece or an accompaniment to that special outfit—and the results are truly stunning.

Known for collecting gemstones from all over the world, Tayma uses aquamarine, rainbow-coloured tourmalines, tanzanite, rubies, sapphires and diamonds from places as diverse as Brazil, South Africa, Myanmar, Madagascar and Sri Lanka. Her own multi-cultural upbringing in Malta, Trinidad and Nigeria initiated her interest in rare gems from these exotic locations. Her passion and hard work have certainly paid off; the result is a stylish and inviting showroom literally glittering in fantastic and vibrant pinks, blues and greens; and with drawers and drawers of sparkling gemstones, it's a treasure chest chock-full of any girl's best friends.

FACTS

PRODUCT custom-designed couture jewellery • ready-to-wear jewellery
FEATURES rare and unusual certificated coloured gemstones and diamonds • personal consultations • worldwide delivery
NEARBY Central • ifc mall • Star Ferry • Mandarin Hotel • Four Seasons Hotel
CONTACT Shop 252, 2nd Floor, Prince's Building, 10 Chater Road, Central, Hong Kong • telephone: +852.2525 5280 • facsimile: +852.2526 1017 • email: finedesign@taymajewellery.com • website: www.taymajewellery.com

PHOTOGRAPHS COURTESY OF TAYMA FINE JEWELLERY.

Times Square

Opened in 1994 on the former site of the Hong Kong Tramway Depot, Times Square is now marked as one of the ten most popular tourist destinations in Hong Kong. Its twin towers rise 46 storeys over Causeway Bay, making it a distinctive landmark in this vibrant shopping district. Surrounded by zig-zagging lanes of small boutiques and lively restaurants, Times Square sits firmly in the centre of the action. Busy during the day with vendors and businessmen, Causeway Bay really comes alive at night. Like many malls in Hong Kong, Times Square provides for these evening shoppers and remains open long after dark. With its focal location, you'll find a buzz here that other malls might lack at this late shopping hour.

Times Square's ultra-modern interior houses more than 230 world-renowned brands over 17 floors; each dedicated to a shopping theme that includes fashion, home furnishings, electronics, sports and beauty. A

...you'll find a buzz here that other shopping malls might lack...

sophisticated range of à la mode brands— from French Connection to agnès b., from Birkenstock to Calvin Klein—supplies a diverse market. Lane Crawford, on the ground floor, encompasses the world's most prestigious designers in fashion and cosmetics while smaller boutiques specialise in health and beauty, accessories, jewellery and watches. A floor for sports gear includes Nike, New Balance and Reebok while another is dedicated to beauty brands such as Crabtree and Evelyn. By positioning like-minded brands together Times Square has created a convenient shopping

experience which makes it easy to search for one product or browse through them all. The main seven-floored atrium is finished with a stunning roof, while each floor has unique lighting effects that create a superb environment in which to shop.

On the top floor of the mall, a buzzing food forum quickly regenerates your energy for shopping with a choice of over 20 restaurants. You can indulge in dumplings at Crystal Jade, Italian at California Pizza Kitchen or ice-cream at Häagan Dazs on Basement 2; there is plenty of choice to satisfy your hunger pangs.

Outside, the main square is used as a convenient meeting place and, over time, crowds have chosen it as a public forum to celebrate many of the year's festivals. As a response, Times Square uses its giant video screen to run countdowns for New Year's Eve and other celebrations; and it's always guaranteed to be a lively location to witness Hong Kong's main events.

FACTS

PRODUCTS	fashion • accessories • beauty • sports gear
FOOD	food forum: 20 restaurants with Western and Asian cuisine
DRINK	food forum
FEATURES	events • convenient layout
NEARBY	Causeway Bay • Happy Valley Racecourse • Victoria Park
CONTACT	1 Matheson Street, Causeway Bay, Hong Kong • telephone: +852.2118 8900 • facsimile: +852.2118 8934 • email: tselpro@timessquare.com.hk • website: www.timessquare.com.hk

PHOTOGRAPHS COURTESY OF TIMES SQUARE.

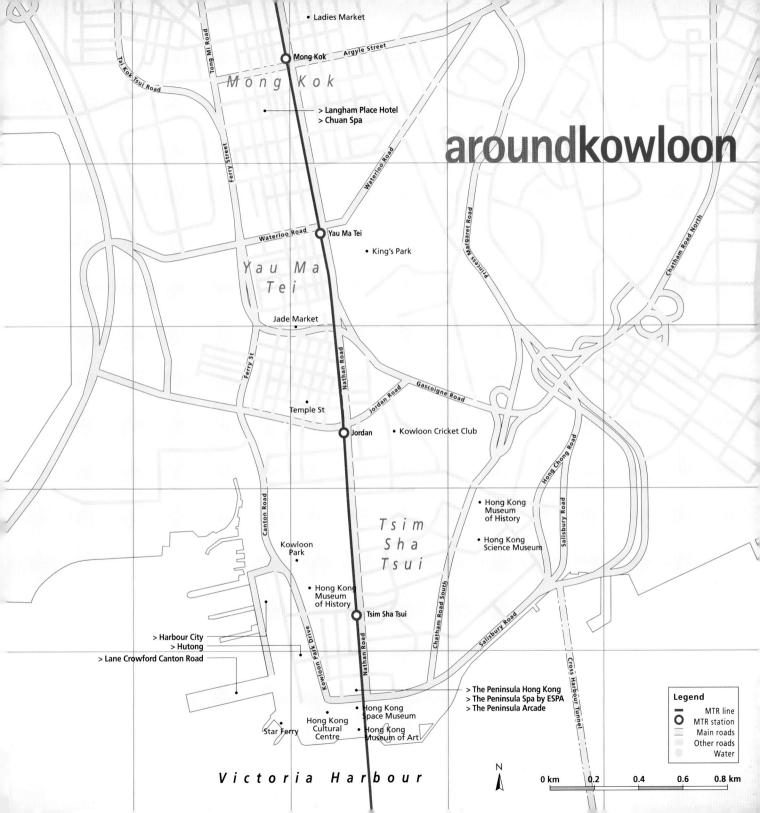

aroundkowloon

- Ladies Market

Mong Kok

Mong Kok

> Langham Place Hotel
> Chuan Spa

Yau Ma Tei

Yau Ma Tei

- King's Park

Jade Market

Temple St

Jordan

- Kowloon Cricket Club

Tsim Sha Tsui

- Hong Kong Museum of History
- Hong Kong Science Museum

Kowloon Park

- Hong Kong Museum of History

Tsim Sha Tsui

> Harbour City
> Hutong
> Lane Crowford Canton Road

> The Peninsula Hong Kong
> The Peninsula Spa by ESPA
> The Peninsula Arcade

Star Ferry

Hong Kong Cultural Centre

- Hong Kong Space Museum

Hong Kong Museum of Art

Victoria Harbour

N

| 0 km | 0.2 | 0.4 | 0.6 | 0.8 km |

Legend

— MTR line
○ MTR station
— Main roads
  Other roads
  Water

say it with flowers

The post-handover flag features a stylised bauhinia, the orchid-like blossom that can be seen everywhere. While it doesn't quite stir the same emotions as the Stars and Stripes, Nisshoki rising sun or Union Jack, it symbolises more than just a decorative replacement of the colonial flag. The bauhinia blakeana is just one example of the flora and fauna native to Hong Kong. It was named after Sir Henry Blake, the botany-advocating governor (1898—1903) whose legacy lives on in more than a single flower.

For a 'barren rock' turned financial metropolis, Hong Kong is surprisingly green, even more so than most residents realise. The government protects about 40 per cent of the total land area from development. That adds up to about 41,482 hectares (10,2500 acres) comprising marshes, woodlands, hills, coastlines and reservoirs. Hikers, athletes and nature enthusiasts make use of the city's 23 country parks and 15 special areas every weekend, if not daily. And that does not even take into account the beautiful beaches along its 733 km (456 miles) of coastline, also caught in the tug of war between urbanisation and efforts to preserve Hong Kong's natural heritage.

all creatures great and small

Tigers, elephants and rhinoceroses once roamed past orchids, camellias and oak trees in Hong Kong's subtropical rainforest ecosystem. Although many were locally extinct by the 20th century, Hong Kong continues to support extraordinary biodiversity thanks to its climate and topography. In some cases, local animal populations make up a significant proportion of their total numbers on the entire globe. The 234 species of butterflies constitute about 20 per cent of all butterfly species found in China. Seven out of the 107 species of dragonfly found here are unique to Hong Kong. There are more vascular plants in the territory than in Great Britain and other countries. Inspiring thousands of bird watchers, Hong Kong has about 488 species of birds, or about one-third of the recorded number in Mainland China.

PAGE 152: A breathtaking aerial view of the New Territories.

THIS PAGE (FROM TOP): The Butterfly House at the Ocean Park; a delicate dragonfly resting on a fence.

OPPOSITE: Hiking trail on Lantau.

for the birds

Bird watching is a popular escape for Hong Kong's urbanites. Many vibrant birds pass through in migration to Siberia and Australia between September and May, making this the best time of year for bird watching. Although bird watching is possible throughout Hong Kong, the rural areas of the northern New Territories offer the best vantage points.

In May 2006, the new Wetland Park was established as a haven for the region's diverse wildlife and to raise awareness of environmental protection. In addition to the 60-hectare (148-acre) man-made reserve, there are other indoor facilities to both entertain and educate people on the importance of conservation.

park life

The government's park system scheme dates back to the 19th century, evidence of which can easily be found in the heart of the city. Established in 1864, the Hong Kong Zoological and Botanical Gardens in Central is where the elderly gather as the sun is rising to practise tai chi, and where children meet on outdoor play dates, racing to find their favourite animals. Perched just above, and formerly part of, the Government House, views of sharp metal skyscrapers through rare trees create a poignant contrast.

There are over 1,000 species of rare plants in the Gardens, carefully labelled for visitors. The calls of the 'orang-utans' can be heard in nearby apartments and office blocks. They live in recently expanded digs alongside gibbons, pythons, tamarins, lemurs and jaguars. The bright pink flamingos always draw a crowd, as do the birds—more than 500 of them—such as the scarlet ibis. Programmes for breeding birds close to extinction have been so successful, the facility supplies them to zoos around the world.

victoria is ours

Victoria Park is Hong Kong's largest public park, stretching over 17 hectares (42 acres) in Causeway Bay. Comparisons with New York's Central Park are inevitable, though not entirely accurate. Constructed on reclaimed land and opened in 1957, it is as grey as it is green but nonetheless a large, open space that is important to the community.

On any given day, you'll witness seniors practising tai chi at dawn, couples relaxing on the grass, intense football matches on cement pitches, and pick-up games of basketball. The world's top ranked tennis players have competed in tournaments on its many tennis courts. There are also squash courts, a swimming pool, and roller skating rink.

This is where the local community meets, whether it's for the annual flower market in the days before Chinese New Year, the Mid-Autumn Festival when children carry beautiful traditional lanterns, or more sobering political demonstrations. Open 24 hours, it also serves as a creative midnight picnic spot for the more adventurous (and patrolling policemen in this remarkably safe city). Kowloon Park and Hong Kong Park are also popular destinations; just a few of the carefully planned public parks scattered across the territory's developed landscape.

take a hike

Escaping to natural settings takes only a matter of minutes in this tiny city. An efficient network of ferries, trains and buses whisk passengers off to outlying islands and remote areas. Victoria Peak, known as The Peak or Tai Ping Shan ('Mountain of Great Peace'), is a short taxi or bus ride from commercial centres such as Central and Wan Chai. On days when pollution is low, the commanding vistas make it easy to understand why The Peak has some of the most exclusive addresses. It stands 552 m (1,811 ft) above sea level, but is not the highest in Hong Kong. That honour

*THIS PAGE: **A spot of tranquillity in a bamboo grove at Tai Lam Country Park.***

OPPOSITE (CLOCKWISE FROM LEFT): A beautiful bauhinia blooms; proud bird owners exhibiting their pets are a common sight in parks; a girl plays near a koi pond in a park.

goes to Tai Mo Shan at 957 m (3,140 ft) in the western New Territories. The Peak's impressive surrounding parks and walking trails are the best ways to experience the natural beauty of Hong Kong.

Following Blake's example, subsequent governors such as Murray Maclehose (1971—1982), helped map out beautiful walking and hiking trails. Hikers of all levels from walkers to serious athletes enjoy the country parks, strolling or running around reservoirs and across the hills. Famous trails include the Dragon's Back, which leads from The Peak to Shek O on the south side of Hong Kong Island; and the Maclehose Trail, from Sai Kung Country Park to Tuen Mun in the New Territories. Taking it to the next level, the trails are now the site of gruelling adventure races, mountain marathons and the famous Oxfam Trailwalker, a charity challenge which involves completing the 100-km (62-mile) Maclehose Trail in less than 48 hours. Local legends and beliefs are attached to numerous spots such as Lover's Rock or Yan Yuen Shek. Located near Happy Valley, it is a shrine where husband-seeking Chinese women to make offerings and burn joss sticks, especially during the Maiden's Festival in August. Little waterfalls and pools are an unexpected bonus in some of these areas.

water works

There are many ways to enjoy the water too, including countless beaches throughout Hong Kong. About 40 of them are gazetted, which means they are cleaned, supervised by lifeguards and often complete with facilities like bathrooms and showers. Surfers make the pilgrimage to places like Tai Long Wan in Sai Kung, and

THIS PAGE: Such profuse greenery balances out the urban sprawl.
OPPOSITE (FROM TOP): Making waves at one of the many beaches; the lesser known beach life of Hong Kong.

Big Wave Bay on the southern tip of Hong Kong Island; while windsurfers can rent equipment at nearby Stanley or Cheung Chau. Like a Hong Kong version of Seurat's 'La Grande Jatte', beaches such as Repulse Bay are often dotted with hordes of people there to barbecue, chat, and sometimes swim on weekends. For the privileged, there is also a strong boating culture. Junks and yachts take groups out to cleaner waters, which are perfect for a bit of skiing and wakeboarding; sailing regattas too take place regularly.

go fish

Hong Kong has an amazing diversity of marine life. Even though its small territorial waters cover only 5 per cent of the South China Sea, it has a greater variety of fish than the tropical Caribbean.

Nine hundred and eighty-one marine fish species from 134 families and 27 orders can be found; brought here by three separate ocean currents (the Chinese Coastal Current, the South China Sea Drift and the Kuroshio Current) and the Pearl River. These species are sheltered by many different kinds of habitat; helping to ensure their preservation too are four marine parks and one reserve.

for your amusement

For years, Ocean Park on the south side of Hong Kong Island has helped to raise local awareness of marine life and nature. Its Atoll Reef aquarium, the largest of its kind in the Asian region, mesmerises children and adults with more than 2,000 kinds of tropical fish, sharks and sea creatures.

It's also famous for performances by sea lions and dolphins, as well as two giant pandas. Two mountains are connected by bubble-shaped cable cars; and rollercoasters were brought in during the 1980s to draw larger crowds. The 2005 opening of Hong Kong Disneyland was feared as a threat to its survival, but has only helped to raise visitor numbers.

Hong Kong's indigenous Chinese White Dolphins (also found in the seas from South Africa to Australia) have become a tourist attraction for their pink appearance. Tours run by Hong Kong Dolphinwatch around Lantau highlight the need to maintain the delicate balance in the ecosystem for these remarkable mammals. For example, dredging for the construction of the massive Chek Lap Kok airport on Lantau posed a serious threat to their survival in the South China Sea.

green day

It isn't easy being green in a financially-motivated city. Hong Kong's ecosystem has been depleted by pollution and rapid urbanisation. While dense housing used to be confined to a few urban areas, rural areas such as Ting Chung on Lantau have now been developed into new towns, and other outlying islands have been targeted for large infrastructure projects.

The booming area of Sha Tin, for example, was farmland just 20 years ago. There are now more cars on the roads due to improvements in the standard of living, which not only increases air and noise pollution but also the amount of traffic in the countryside.

The outlook, however, is not entirely bleak. The government has spent a great deal of money on green initiatives. After the majority of Hong Kong's tropical trees were chopped down for cooking fuel during the Japanese Occupation, Australian eucalyptus and other non-native plants were planted to replace them. In recent years, planting efforts in urban areas have brightened the city's 'black spots'. Recycling in Hong Kong, although not practised or enforced as strongly as in other major cities of the world, is on the rise.

The city is looking into more environmentally-friendly, renewable energy sources such as wind farms. Hong Kongers are slowly changing the way they view urban development and environmental issues. And, believe it or not, a few species of fish have proven that life is returning to the famous harbour.

THIS PAGE (FROM TOP): A group of brightly glowing moon jellyfish pulse through the sea; anchored boats awaiting their next weekend outing. OPPOSITE: Flights of fancy at Ocean Park.

believe it or not

More than 600 temples and shrines dotted throughout Hong Kong reveal the community's main spiritual beliefs—a complex system of Buddhism, Taoism and other Chinese traditions. Luck, prosperity and longevity are key, as demonstrated by various practices. Fortune-tellers, often set up in or around temples, are still consulted and addressed with more respect that the carnival gypsies of Western cultures. It is not unusual to meet business people clad in designer labels, then catch a glimpse of a jade talisman hanging from a chain around their necks or a set of crystal bead bracelets next to the Cartier watch on their wrists.

A purer form of Feng Shui, rather than the watered-down kind recently touted by pop culture and Hollywood, is still practised here. Feng Shui masters are often called in to offices and new residences to help balance the natural elements and ward off evil spirits.

rise and shrine

Several religious structures date back 700 years while others are more recent. Among them are the extremely popular Wong Tai Sin Temple in Kowloon (named after a Taoist deity of giving); Chi Nin Nunnery and a group of temples built in Tang dynasty-style architecture on Diamond Hill; Po Lin Monastery on Lantau island with the famous giant bronze statue of Tian Tan Buddha; Che Kung Temple in Sha Tin; and Man Mo Temple on Hong Kong Island.

Tin Hau, the Queen of Heaven and protector of seafarers, has a large following and over 24 temples in her name—understandable for a territory that has always been dependent on the sea. Kwun Yum, the Buddhist Goddess of Mercy, is also extremely popular among Taoists and Buddists.

Besides places of worship, many major religious groups have established schools, community facilities and charitable outreach programmes to perpetuate their faith through education and charity work.

THIS PAGE: Over 200 steps lead up to the Tian Tan Buddha on Lantau island.

OPPOSITE (FROM TOP): Christianity—one of the many threads in Hong Kong's religious fabric; the lotus flower is an important Buddhist symbol of purity.

free to be

Religious freedom in Hong Kong has allowed various beliefs to flourish. About 10 per cent of the population is Christian. There are approximately 61 churches and chapels in Hong Kong. Islam has been practised in the territory since the late 19th century; the Jamia Mosque on Shelley Street was originally constructed in the 1840s. Hinduism and Sikhism are also prominent, and Judaism in China and Hong Kong has a long and interesting history.

come on now

There are countless religious festivals throughout the year. Colourful, noisy community gatherings that often include firecrackers, bright paper effigies, and lion or dragon dances. The most important festival is Chinese New Year (also known as Lunar New Year). Held in January or February, depending on the lunar calendar, this is the one

time of year when the city actually slows down to celebrate. For three days or more, people visit families and friends. Unmarried people and children receive red lai see or 'lucky money' packets filled with crisp new bills. Symbolic sweets and snacks auger luck, prosperity and good fortune for the new year. In celebration of the important holiday, the government stages firework displays over the harbour. Vibrant flower markets are set up in prominent areas such as Victoria Park to supply homes with new blooms including cherry blossoms and narcissus. White, the colour of death, is avoided. At Sha Tin Racecourse, a special lion dance and Chinese New Year Cup race is held annually. Temples are at their busiest, with people swarming to give thanks and praying for good fortune in the year ahead.

ghosts of the past

In spring, the Ching Ming Festival (translated as 'bright and clear') is a time for families to visit and tidy ancestral graves. Ancestral worship is also observed in autumn, during the Chung Yeung Festival. Families make offerings and pay their respects at the graves of departed relatives, often situated in remote country areas. In the late summer, it is believed that the doors to the underworld open up and release 'angry ghosts' who have been forgotten, or whose spirits of those whose descendents have failed to look after their graves, or who were buried without funeral rites. The Hungry Ghost Festival is held to pacify the roaming spirits with elaborate roadside effigies, paper burning ceremonies and sometimes, Cantonese opera performances.

by the light of the silvery moon

For children, the Mid-Autumn Festival is a time to choose from a dazzling array of vibrant lanterns in animal shapes such as the classic gold and orange goldfish. Although previously handmade from paper and lit from within by a small candle, lanterns are today usually made of plastic in cartoon character forms with battery operated lights. Celebrations include visits to parks at night to view the moon and

THIS PAGE (FROM TOP):
During major festivals, believers take to the streets to burn joss sticks and paper effigies; plastic lanterns sold during the Mid-Autumn Festival.
OPPOSITE: A scramble up a tower of buns during the Cheung Chau Bun Festival.

parade one's lantern. The exchanging of mooncakes is an essential part of the festivities; a tradition which stems from a 14th-century uprising against the Mongols. Messages on pieces of paper were hidden inside cakes and smuggled to allies. Mooncakes are traditionally made from pastry and lotus seed paste with an egg yolk in the middle, but modern innovations have now introduced a plethora of different types such as mooncakes made from ice-cream.

baker's dozen

Cheung Chau Bun Festival in April or May is a truly unique spectacle. Staged on the small island of Cheung Chau, the festival features enormous towers constructed from bamboo frames covered in white buns near Pak Tai Temple. Its origins are debatable, but the activities are generally believed to chase away evil spirits. Children participate in a procession, wearing bright costumes and parading through the streets on stilts. The event climaxes with climbers, mostly men, scrambling up the towers to grab as many of the steamed buns as they can.

row, row, row

In early summer, The Dragon Boat Festival (Tuen Ng) commemorates Chu Yuen, a 4th-century scholar and poet who drowned himself in protest against corruption in the government. When he was buried at sea, his friends threw dumplings into the water and pounded on drums to prevent the fish from eating his body. Today, it has become a

boisterous community-wide celebration spanning all cultures. Crews of various levels of skill and dedication, including corporate teams, compete in races off Aberdeen, Stanley, Sha Tin, Tai Po, Cheung Chau and Lantau. They consist of 18 to 20 forward-facing paddlers who row to the rhythm of a drummer positioned at the bow, near the dragon head. At the stern or tail of the 15-m (49-ft) boat is a helmsman who steers with a fixed oar. Dragon boat races attract hoards of spectators and are a major social event, fuelled by customary treats such as glutinous rice wrapped in bamboo leaves and, today, beer.

be a sport

At the 1996 Atlanta Olympic Games, Lee Lai Shan—the windsurfer from Cheung Chau island more affectionately known as San San—won Hong Kong its first ever gold medal since the city joined the Olympics in 1952. The city has homegrown world-class professional athletes and medallists in diverse disciplines such as table tennis, squash, badminton, swimming, cycling, triathlon, rock climbing, horse racing, and more. It is a great achievement, considering physical education in schools often takes a backseat to exam preparation or simply because a lack of space. Nevertheless, there are myriad ways to enjoy sports. Tai chi is practised in the early hours of the morning in urban and country parks. Countless beautiful hiking trails invite walkers and runners. Elegant country and golf clubs have waiting lists that stretch not for months but years. The government manages over 1,500 sports grounds and centres. Associations and amateur competitions also highlight opportunities for getting active. Even more impressive is Hong Kong's calendar of international sporting events.

give it a try

What started in 1976 as a little event for the lesser known form of rugby has become an international extravaganza held annually in late March or early April. The Hong Kong Sevens now sells out the 40,000-seat Hong Kong Stadium, leaving fans scrambling for last-minute tickets or much-prized passes into the corporate sponsor

THIS PAGE (FROM TOP): After months of training, teams compete in traditional boats at the annual dragon boat races; crowds gather to watch these fiercely competitive dragon boat races.

OPPOSITE (FROM LEFT): The raucous south stand is always entertaining at the Hong Kong Sevens; exciting action on the field during a game.

Horse racing is an integral part of Hong Kong culture.

boxes. Over the three-day weekend, about 24 teams representing countries across the globe compete for three trophies: the cup, plate and bowl. As the championship has grown, other events for men, women and children have been added to the programme. The exhilarating atmosphere is further charged by the wild south stand, where the rowdiest fans congregate, often in fancy dress. When the matches are over, the festive atmosphere moves from the grounds to party tents and the nightlife districts.

hold your horses

Horse racing is an integral part of Hong Kong culture. Fuelling a local obsession, gambling appeals across socio-economic levels from taxi drivers to tycoons. In fact, it is so profitable that the non-profit Hong Kong Jockey Club's massive annual contributions help to keep the population's income taxes low. The season lasts from September to June or early July, with races at its two racecourses on most Wednesday nights and weekends. On those days, local television is dominated by horse racing coverage. Built on reclaimed marshland, the Happy Valley Racecourse hosted its first events in 1846, with night races introduced in 1973. The track now has high-tech accoutrements such as massive screens on which to broadcast the races, and computerised betting systems. Based on the success of Happy Valley, a second racecourse was opened in Sha Tin in 1978. Its giant video screen is as long as a 747 airplane, and is listed as the longest television display in the world according to the Guinness Book of World Records.

Hong Kong's horse racing world is so advanced, it has been selected to host and oversee the three-day equestrian events of the 2008 Beijing Olympic Games. The facilities attract other international events such as the Hong Kong Derby, the Queen Elizabeth II Cup and the Hong Kong International Races. With the world's richest purses for first prize, the best horses and jockeys arrive from around the world to join in the race. For recreational riders, there are several riding clubs on both sides of the harbour which also provide homes to retired racehorses.

THIS PAGE (FROM TOP): **The Hong Kong Jockey Club's racing museum in Happy Valley; jockeys are stars in this horse racing obsessed society.**
OPPOSITE:
Thoroughbreds thundering down the race track.

The Hong Kong Jockey Club also has a racing museum at the Happy Valley Racecourse. Opened on October 18, 1996, the museum chronicles the history of the club, horse racing in Hong Kong and more. The venue is also used to host events and projects for charity, an important role that the Hong Kong Jockey Club has held to great effect over the years.

goal!

Another Hong Kong passion is football. The local professional league has a strong following, while rivalries are also played out by amateur or weekend leagues with several divisions and a recorded point scoring system. In addition to local teams, expatriates have joined in the fun, usually teaming up with fellow countrymen. At Chinese New Year, fanatics can gamble away their entire lai see takings on the New Year Soccer Cup. Over two days, three famous international teams and a team of Hong Kong's best compete for the title.

To tackle the problem of illegal betting, the government decided to legalise it in 2003 and providing the Hong Kong Jockey Club, already managing the territory's horse racing gambling and Mark Six lottery, with the only license.

wicket ways

A colonial remnant, cricket has been played in Hong Kong since 1841. Today, some of the world's best cricket players return annually for the Hong Kong International Cricket Sixes which began in 1992. Like the Rugby Sevens, the Cricket Sixes have put Hong Kong on the sport's international calendar with a previously little-known version of the game. Through the Hong Kong Cricket Association and the Sports Development Board, the sport has been brought to different age groups and genders. With dedicated cricket clubs on both sides of the harbour, a Saturday league and a Sunday league, the various cricket teams actively compete, particularly in the cooler months between September to April.

match point

Tennis is a popular social activity that has been played in Hong Kong as far back as 1909. According to the Tennis Association, there are over 8,000 registered players and 600 tennis courts, public tennis facilities and prestigious private clubs. For years, junior teams have toured overseas, and a Davis Cup team has competed in the international competition since 1970. The Tennis Patrons' Association, founded in 1976, helped secure professional tennis events and supports the development of junior talent. Most recently, the annual Champions Challenge has drawn in stars of women's tennis, including the likes of Venus and Serena Williams, Lindsay Davenport, and Kim Clijsters.

join the club

Other racquet sports also thrive in Hong Kong. The table tennis duo of Ko Lai Chak and Li Ching captured silver medals at the 2004 Athens Olympic Games; badminton players Amy Chan and Chan Chi Choi took home the bronze from the 1988 Seoul Olympics. The Hong Kong Open Badminton Championships brings together 200 of the sport's elite from 30 different countries. Similarly, the Hong Kong World Squash Open is a big draw. The event is held towards the end of the year in cooler weather, which allows stunts such as staging the semi-finals and finals in a four-sided clear squash court right at the harbour-front outside the Hong Kong Cultural Centre.

marathon sessions

When we say Hong Kong is constantly on the move, we mean it. Runners take on the heat and the hills, joining mountain marathons, aquathons, triathlons and social 'hashes'. The Hong Kong Marathon is reputedly the largest sporting event in the city, pulling together 30,000 runners both local and visiting. Trailing from the centre of Kowloon to the Tsing Ma Bridge and across to Hong Kong Island, it is also the final leg of the four-marathon, cross-continental 'Greatest Race on Earth'.

THIS PAGE: *The Hong Kong Marathon is also the final leg of the 'Greatest Race on Earth'.*

OPPOSITE (FROM LEFT): *Local and international football matches are closely followed; cricket has a dedicated following in Hong Kong.*

to a tee

Played here before anywhere else in the Far East, golf has become particularly popular in the past 40 years. The Hong Kong Golf Club is one of the 100 oldest in the world. In 1968, the Hong Kong Golf Association was established to encourage and promote the sport through championships and training. Inspiring stories of local stars include numerous former caddies who went on to compete at international level. Previously limited to privileged expatriates, the creation of public facilities such as the Tuen Mun Driving Range and the Kau Sai Chau Public Golf Course have helped popularise the game. Players from the European and Asian tours join the annual Hong Kong Open, Asia's second-longest running golf tournament.

in the swim

It's easy to get to the water from any of Hong Kong's series of islands, and people often do. While some choose to frolic by a beach, others dive into more energetic aquatic pursuits such as windsurfing, sea kayaking, wakeboarding, water skiing and, to the surprise of many, even surfing. The first yacht race in the territory was recorded in 1849; just the beginning of what continues to be a fanatically followed activity and a tight-knit community. The Royal Hong Kong Yacht Club, for example, organises a full calendar of races and regattas from its three clubhouses scattered around the territory. One of the legendary sources of tales and experiences to recount is the China Sea Race. Co-organised with the Manila Yacht Club, it starts from Hong Kong's Victoria Harbour and continues across the South China Sea to Subic Bay in the Philippines.

a city in motion

If potholes are signs of a city in financial straits, then Hong Kong's remarkably clean, affordable and reliable transport system is surely proof of its prosperity. A network of trains, ferries, buses, taxis and trams connect the territory's islands, making it possible to go from the clattering urban jungle into undeveloped wilderness in a matter of minutes.

THIS PAGE (FROM TOP):
Not just a game for the privileged anymore, golf is now easily accessible to anyone; Tsing Ma Bridge, one of the world's longest suspension bridges, connects Kowloon with Lantau island.

OPPOSITE: Public swimming pools make it possible for everyone to take a dip.

Where the land ends, cross-harbour tunnels and extraordinary bridges fill in the gaps, such as Tsing Ma Bridge, one of the world's longest suspension bridges. And you won't find rickety old rickshaws crossing them either. Hong Kong possesses some of the most luxury cars per capita.

The people still drive on the left, following the British rules of the road, and street signs are in both traditional Chinese characters and English. Reminders of the past aside, it seems the city is constantly under construction, from the bamboo-style

scaffolding on new skyscrapers to the ever-present cacophony of jackhammers on some part of its road. Racing forward, Hong Kong has employed modern technology to only not maintain old icons, but also to introduce newer ways to move its people.

ferry tales

The quaint rickshaw may have been relegated to something tourists like to take pictures with, but other charming, nostalgic forms of transport remain in operation. The Kowloon Ferry Company, founded by an entrepreneurial Parsee named Dorabjee Nowrojee, began shuttling passengers between Hong Kong Island and Kowloon in 1888. It was given its more famous name, the Star Ferry, in 1898, and still offers some of the best views of the harbour, especially at night. Connecting Central, Wan Chai, Tsim Sha Tsui and Hung Hom, each vessel in the Star Ferry fleet has 'star' in her name, such as 'Morning Star'. Just as enthusiastic photo snapping might indicate a tour group is aboard, formally dressed passengers usually suggest there's an evening performance in one of the harbour-front cultural complexes. The short journey is a pleasant, open-air alternative to road or underground cross-harbour passage, with an air-conditioned cabin on the upper deck for steamy summer days. Land reclamation has claimed the old Star Ferry pier in Central, so it will be moved to the outlying islands ferry piers a few hundred metres to the west.

Hong Kong has a long maritime history. With one of the world's busiest container ports, shipping has contributed to the territory's economic success and the fortunes of an elite group of magnates. Travelling by boat is, in fact, a daily exercise for many Hong Kongers. A number of ferry companies convey commuters and visitors to the outlying islands and beyond. High-speed boats head for Macau and into China. Affordable cruise ships leave Hong Kong waters for overnight gambling trips, or short jaunts to nearby areas.

The traditional Chinese junk with its distinctive sails used to be a symbol of Hong Kong; and the last remaining example, Duk Ling, is still seen cruising the harbour on Thursdays and Saturdays as part of a Hong Kong Tourism Board programme. The grand old wooden boats may have retired; but a renowned restaurant group, Aqua, recently went through the painstaking process of recreating the traditional junk, and now offers exclusive, catered harbour cruises.

got cable?

Back ashore, trams on Hong Kong Island provide another practical form of transport that has become a tourist attraction. The idea of transporting residents and their employees from Central to prestigious residences on The Peak was proposed by the enterprising Alexander Findlay-Smith in 1881.

The common mode of transport at the time was the sedan chair, a bamboo seat supported on the shoulders of two unfortunate coolies (the colonial term for labourers). The repeated, gruelling uphill trek in a hot, humid climate sounds like a task only Sisyphus could have endured—carrying passengers up and down from about 28 m (92 ft) above sea level near Central to about 396 m (1,299 ft) above sea level at Victoria Peak. A charity sedan chair race now takes place on The Peak every year with contestants often dressed in fanciful costumes.

The Peak Tram, wooden and powered by coal-fired steam boilers, was officially opened in May 1888 by Governor Sir George William Des Voeux. For over 40 years, a brass plaque on the first two seats of the tramcar read, 'This seat is reserved for His Excellency, The Governor.' Eventually, class distinctions faded and electric power replaced steam. By 1989, the systems were computerised, and the tramcars were constructed in lightweight metal. Today, the double-reversible funicular railway climbs about 373 m (1,224 ft), pulled by steel cables along its track, presenting views and an experience that have visitors lining up around the block.

THIS PAGE (CLOCKWISE FROM TOP): A funicular Peak Tram which ascends to The Peak; residents rely on an efficient network of buses, trams and trains to get around; quaint modes of transport are still in use, thanks to advertisers who add their signature looks to street trams.
OPPOSITE: Road signs are made in English and Chinese.

on the tracks

There is something comforting in relics that survive the relentless pace of modernisation. Street trams continue to operate along a 13-km (8-mile) main line that runs on the east-west axis of northern Hong Kong Island. So do modern buses, taxis and subways. Yet the trams carry 240,000 passengers each day and are so full at rush hours, it's impossible to push past their old-fashioned turnstiles to get on.

Founded in 1904, Hong Kong Tramways now boasts the world's largest fleet of double-deck tramcars, with 163 trams in operation (including two antiques). They also claimed to keep pollution to a minimum thanks to their thermit welding technology. There were originally two conductors selling tickets on each tram. In 1976, drop-in coin boxes were installed and, by 1982, the conductor system was abolished. Most of the conductors were trained to become motormen instead.

Sitting on the upper deck is a wonderful way to view the city's diverse districts. In true Hong Kong fashion, these Old-World modes of transport have found extra revenue streams through rentals for parties and as attention-grabbing advertisements, temporarily emblazoned with famous logos.

beam me up

Still, Hong Kong's relentless quest to be bigger, better and newer sets the tone in all its developments. What was once an exhausting walk or a harrowing drive up to see the famous Buddha on Lantau has been transformed by the new Ngong Ping Skyrail. The 6-km (4-mile), 25-minute cable car journey takes passengers from Tung Chung up to Ngong Ping in 17-person cabins, offering at the same time breathtaking views of northern Lantau's greenery.

Then again, some prefer to walk. Constructed in the 1990s, The Mid-Levels Escalator is the world's longest covered escalator, spanning 800 m (2,625 ft) from Central to Mid-Levels. In the mornings, it brings office workers, students and market shoppers down the hill. In the afternoons and evenings, it takes them back up.

networking

Though less of a novelty, Hong Kong's network of taxis, buses and trains is quite possibly the cleanest, most efficient and affordable of any major city. The single- and double-decker buses of the Kowloon Motor Bus Co. Ltd, New World First Bus Services Ltd, Citybus, and the New Lantao Bus Co. cover most of Hong Kong Island, Kowloon, the New Territories, and Lantau. Green and yellow Maxicabs take specific routes with set fares which are paid upon entry. Red and yellow minibuses may stop anywhere for passengers except bus stops, and payment comes at the end of the journey.

Whereas a ride in a London taxi is a planned treat for most, the metered Toyotas of Hong Kong are extremely reasonable. The best-known taxis are red and service Hong Kong Island and the urban areas of Kowloon. Green taxis can be found in the New Territories and charge less than their red sisters. The cheapest cover Lantau and are blue.

*THIS PAGE (FROM TOP):
Everything is on the move as a
blur of traffic is reflected in a
pedestrian light;
taxi drivers are the unofficial
ambassadors of the city.*

*OPPOSITE: Millions travel daily on
the MTR—a lone passenger
takes time out to watch the
trains go by.*

rail time

There are two railway systems in Hong Kong—the Kowloon-Canton Railway (KCR) and the Mass Transit Railway (MTR). Founded in 1910 as a single track system, the KCR provides light rail rapid transit service within towns of Tuen Mun and Yuen Long, in addition to a commuter train service in the New Territories and into Mainland China.

The MTR is one of the most impressive in the world. The trains are clean; routes are clearly marked in Chinese and English; and the walls are in a different colour in each station. Opened in 1979, the MTR now has various lines that zip to the outer reaches of Hong Kong and run over 84 km (52 miles) through 51 stations. One of the fastest ways to move around the city, the MTR carries about 2.4 million passengers every weekday. The well-planned Airport Express stations take convenience to the next level and even allow in-town check-in with major airlines.

Trains, once a symbol of modern times, are again associated with future progress as the KCR and MTR are set to merge. The new era is significant not only for Hong Kong, but also for its growing closeness to Mainland China.

The MTR is one of the most impressive in the world.

Trains towards Sheun

Langham Place Hotel

Only 15 minutes from the Star Ferry pier on Kowloon is Mong Kok, one of the more lively and vibrant regions of Hong Kong. Colourful markets dominate the area, and a constant mass of jostling locals creates a spirited atmosphere. Here you'll find everything from the Goldfish Market to the Ladies Market. (Don't be deceived by the latter's name, however. It's full of knick-knacks and clothing for both men and women.) Towering above these sidestreets and alleyways is a metropolis unto itself, Langham Place.

Occupying 42 floors, Langham Place Hotel is a refreshing and calming contrast to the frenetic energy on the streets outside. The rooms and suites are modern and luxurious, each offering all the state-of-the-art amenities expected of a five-star hotel. Upon arrival in your suite, the stunning glass-walled bathroom immediately strikes you with its centrepeice, a huge marble bath. Later, while relaxing in the tub you can enjoy the spectacular views through the floor-to-ceiling windows across Kowloon.

THIS PAGE (FROM TOP): A studio room with floor-to-ceiling windows giving 180° view of the world outside, it makes lying on the Blissful Bed an even greater experience; the rooftop pool, featuring underwater music and lights.

OPPOSITE (FROM LEFT): The cleverly placed bath is the perfect spot to lie back and take in the view; the hotel's lobby greets guests with a sophisticated charm.

...a refreshing and calming contrast to the frenetic energy on the streets outside.

If the nearby markets haven't worn you out, there's a 15-storey entertainment complex within Langham Place. The mall houses over 300 shops, 50 restaurants and a cinema complex; it's guaranteed to satisfy any residual shopping desires—this is, after all, Hong Kong. For those ready to collapse, the rooftop pool is a perfect sun-trap. Or, for the ultimate indulgence, retreat to Chuan Spa for some serious pampering.

Langham Place Hotel offers some diverse culinary experiences from traditional Cantonese at Ming Court to barbecued steak under fairy-lit trees in The Backyard. The Portal, a concept work-and-play area, is a magical hideout for any multi-tasking businessman who likes to enjoy a beer while watching a football game and catching up with the day's emails all at the same time.

If you need to stay in touch with the world twenty-four-seven, the hotel has an astonishing 4,000 network connections, 1,500 IP phones and 500 wireless access points to allow you to do just that. With mobile land phones working anywhere inside the hotel, you can keep connected while eating at any of the restaurants, working out at the fitness studio, or even while lounging by the rooftop pool. Wireless Internet installed throughout the hotel offers guests the opportunity to take their work outdoors and make the most of the panoramic views. Touch-screen phones in the rooms enable guests to access weather updates, the news and stock quotes; and a huge plasma screen with a DVD player (complimentary DVDs available) ensure the hotel's status as the most technologically advanced in the Asia Pacific.

That's not to say the Langham is all cable and wireless. It's also been voted the 'Best Art Gallery Masquerading as a Hotel'; and as Hong Kong's first modern Chinese Art Hotel offering guided art tours, it houses one of the largest collections in the city with over 1,500 pieces from local and Mainland Chinese artists. With such a cultural backdrop, a stay here is always a pleasure.

ROOMS	665
FOOD	The Place: international cuisine • The Backyard: barbeque and grill • Ming Court: Cantonese • Contemplation Corner: refreshments
DRINK	Portal - Work & Play
FEATURES	rooftop pool and jacuzzi • Chuan Spa • fitness studio • wireless Internet • limousine service • walking tour
BUSINESS	business centre • boardrooms
NEARBY	Langham Place Mall • markets • Star Ferry on Kowloon side • Northern Territories
CONTACT	555 Shanghai Street, Mong Kok, Kowloon • telephone: +852.3552 3388 • facsimile: +852.3552 3322 • e-mail: hkg.lph.info@langhamhotels.com • website: http://hongkong.langhamplacehotels.com

The Peninsula Hong Kong

In keeping with the traditions of the finest hospitality, the hotel's impeccable service begins as soon as you land at the airport. In the most glamorous of airport transfers, guests can take a trip back in time with an original 1934 vintage Rolls-Royce Phantom. For guests who want a more modern-day exhilaration, the hotel's helicopter service can whisk them in minutes from the airport to the beautifully appointed China Clipper, a private lounge for helicopter passengers.

Rooms are classical and grand with luxurious silks, heavy-set curtains and an elegant living area. Deluxe marble bathrooms feature a television so you can enjoy a film while enjoying a soak in the deep marble bath. Each room features a CD and DVD player with a library of over 500 titles. The Garden Suite features a terrace;

In a city that holds little nostalgia for its colourful past, The Peninsula Hong Kong is an institution that should definitely not be missed during any trip to Hong Kong. Opened in 1928, the 'Grande Dame of the Far East' is the oldest hotel in Hong Kong and, to this day, is hailed as one of the finest in the world.

Keeping one foot firmly in the grandeur of its history, the other in the comfort of the 21st century, The Peninsula offers unsurpassed surroundings with all the conveniences of state-of-the-art technology.

THIS PAGE (FROM TOP): The majestic exterior of the hotel; expect inventive cuisine and décor at the hip Felix restaurant.

OPPOSITE (FROM LEFT): A Deluxe Harbour View Suite featuring separate sitting and bedroom areas, where guests are treated to a 270° view of the harbour; The Peninsula Suite, offering ultimate luxury with a private balcony, mini-gym, office, and two separate sitting areas.

...one foot firmly in the grandeur of its history, the other in the comfort of the 21st century...

while The Peninsula Suite benefits from a private balcony and telescope to enjoy the postcard panorama of Hong Kong Island, a butler and use of the Rolls-Royce fleet.

Throughout its distinguished past, The Peninsula has welcomed and entertained stars such as Clark Gable and Charlie Chaplin. The lobby's grand pillars, arched windows and palm trees fluttering in copper urns, create a stunning colonial setting for afternoon tea. The kitchen bakes an astounding 1,000 scones every day to cater for its guests. The Peninsula Hong Kong is also home to other long-standing institutions including Gaddi's, one of Hong Kong's finest and best-loved restaurants. Its chandeliers, blue and gold tones, and mirrored columns create a stylish European backdrop for the delicious gourmet French cuisine.

The spectacular interior of the Felix restaurant, designed by Philippe Starck, is an ultra-modern setting for innovative cuisine. Also, offering Cantonese is the serene Spring Moon, and guests can enjoy Swiss cuisine in the authentic Chesa, sushi in the stylish Imasa, and Mediterranean food at the timeless Verandah. There are no less than seven restaurants within the hotel, each reputed as Hong Kong's best, and many offering the 'Naturally Peninsula' light and healthy menus.

Located on Victoria Harbour, in the very heart of Kowloon, The Peninsula has played an instrumental role in developing Tsim Sha Tsui into the lively shopping and entertainment district it is today. Close to the city's museums, the Star Ferry, and with easy access to the rest of Hong Kong and the outer islands, the hotel is still one of the area's popular tourist destinations.

With a Roman-style pool, an impressive spa and three floors of international boutiques in the Shopping Arcade, The Peninsula offers guests a multitude of distractions within its historic walls.

PHOTOGRAPHS COURTESY OF THE PENINSULA HONG KONG.

FACTS

ROOMS	300
FOOD	Gaddi's: French • Felix: contemporary • The Verandah: Mediterranean • Chesa: Swiss • Spring Moon: Cantonese • Imasa: Japanese • Pool Terrace • The Lobby
DRINK	The Lobby • The Bar • Felix
FEATURES	indoor pool • The Peninsula Spa by ESPA • fitness centre • hair salon • afternoon tea • Rolls-Royce service • helicopter services • China Clipper helicopter waiting lounge
BUSINESS	business centre • meeting rooms • banquet facilities • private boardroom • high-tech audio-visual equipment • wired and wireless high-speed Internet access • meeting packages
NEARBY	Star Ferry • Cultural Centre • Museum of Art • Space Museum • Museum of History
CONTACT	Salisbury Road, Kowloon, Hong Kong • telephone: +852.2920 2888 • facsimile: +852.2722 4170 • email: phk@peninsula.com • website: www.peninsula.com

Chuan Spa

With a location on the 40th floor of the Langham Place Hotel, where it enjoys spectacular views across Kowloon, a stunning interior and a vast menu of over 60 luxurious treatments all rooted in traditional Chinese medicine (TCM), Chuan Spa is a Hong Kong highlight not to be missed.

Chinese medicine dates back almost 5,000 years to a time when people lived close to nature and the changing seasons. Now, in the concrete jungle of Hong Kong, where the multitude dash from one air-conditioned block to another, Chuan Spa uses the concept of Wu Xing—the five elements—to help you regain your inherent balance with nature. Using the power of wood, earth, metal, fire and water together with TCM techniques, Chuan Spa addresses each visitor individually and combines therapies and essential oils to ensure you leave refreshed, re-energised and re-aligned with your natural harmony.

The spa offers all conceivable forms of holistic pampering. Having shopped until you dropped, some reflexology will help you recharge; or, for a full-body experience, go for Chuan's wrap treatments. For example, your entire body can be wrapped in soothing warm mud. After working its magic on your skin, the mud is washed away along with the day's stresses. You're left feeling completely revived with radiant, soft skin.

Chuan Spa packages include jet-lag recovery, detoxing and bridal pampering, and their signature treatments focus on re-balancing with the use of acupressure and hot stone techniques. Practising the art of chromatherapy, Chuan Spa's infinity suite is the ultimate pleasure dome. While you unwind in the infinity bath and whirlpool, coloured lights strobe over your body leaving you to take in the healing and invigorating effects. Each colour has its own healing energy—choose violet to seek enlightenment, indigo for calm or red to energise.

Before your treatment begins be sure to make the most of Chuan Spa's stunning facilities and enjoy a sauna, steam room or an Oriental hot tub. Afterwards you can relax with tea in the Contemplation Corner. There's also the superb rooftop outdoor pool and fitness room at your disposal. It's very easy to spend the day luxuriating here.

For the final indulgence, Chuan Spa offers quite an unforgettable pedicure. On the 40th floor, encircled by a floor-to-ceiling window, relaxing in a large heated leather armchair, you'll find yourself mesmerised by the dazzling sight of Kowloon and Victoria Harbour as your feet are splendidly restored for another day of shopping.

FACTS

TREATMENTS	massage • scrubs • manicures • pedicures • reflexology • acupressure • hydrotherapy • chromatherapy
FOOD	Contemplation Corner: spa cuisine
DRINK	Contemplation Corner: tea
FEATURES	sauna • steam room • Oriental hot tubs • outdoor pool • fitness centre • spa boutique
NEARBY	Langham Place Mall • markets • Star Ferry on Kowloon side • Northern Territories
CONTACT	Langham Place Hotel, Level 41, 555 Shanghai Street, Mong Kok, Kowloon • telephone: +852.3552 3510 • facsimile: +852.3552 3529 • email: hkg.lph.info@chuanspa.com • website: www.chuanspa.com

PHOTOGRAPHS COURTESY OF CHUAN SPA.

The Peninsula Spa by ESPA

Located on the 7th and 9th floors of The Peninsula Hong Kong, The Peninsula Spa by ESPA is one of Hong Kong's most luxurious spa facilities. Indeed the spa is in keeping with the hotel's reputation for glamour, first-class service and design.

Beautiful and calming, the spa is decorated with Chinese silk bedspreads, reclaimed wooden floors, cooling mosaic tiles and glassed walls giving views across Hong Kong Island. Original pieces of art, and vases of fragrant tropical flowers fill the rooms. Influences from Dornbracht and Duravit, alongside custom-made beds and lighting, create a striking background for some pampering.

Created by ESPA, the world's leading spa consultancy, The Peninsula Spa is the first of its kind to open in Asia. As part of The Peninsula Hotels' 'Peninsula Wellness' programme to indulge guests' senses both during their stay and beyond, ESPA combines ancient and modern therapies from around the world, in particular from China, India and Europe. It uses their respected philosophies of health and well-being to create cutting-edge treatments for relaxation and rejuvenation along with specialist therapies.

On the specialist menu are pre- and post-natal treatments, anti-cellulite exfoliations, aromatherapy and cleansing back massages. With Hong Kong's most

The Peninsula Spa by ESPA is one of Hong Kong's most luxurious spa facilities.

THIS PAGE (FROM TOP): An intricate lamp adds texture to the spa's décor; the Asian Tea Lounge for pre- and post-treatment relaxation. OPPOSITE (FROM LEFT): Part of the spa services on offer is a private spa experience for two; other facilities also include a Roman-style pool that leads onto the landscaped sun terrace.

vigorous training programme, ESPA staff have unparalleled experience in all the therapies on offer—from holistic body massages to skin firming facials.

Starting with an aromatic tea in the Asian Tea Lounge, guests can luxuriate in a range of healing and cooling experiences to cleanse and relax before treatment begins. Crystal steam rooms, showers, an ice fountain and harbour view saunas are the perfect induction to the pampering which follows. Signature therapies take care of the yin or yang, or any ayurvedic dosha in need of some attention. Outstanding treatments such as 'The Peninsula Ceremonies' indulge guests with a fresh ginger foot buff, a salt and oil body scrub and wrap, an intensive oil and hot stone massage, and a cleansing facial.

The Peninsula Spa also encompasses a huge and inviting Roman-style pool with a waterfall flowing into the pool, huge marble pillars and a glass roof. After a swim, head out onto the landscaped sun terrace to take in the breathtakingly beautiful view of Victoria Harbour and Hong Kong Island.

There is a hair salon on the same floor that offers pedicure and manicure services for further pampering. With a staff-to-guest ratio of 3.5 to 1, you will feel the benefits of The Peninsula Spa's pampering service wherever you are, whether you are in a treatment room or Asian Tea Lounge, where black lychee, chrysanthemum and oolong teas will be served.

FACTS		
ROOMS	14 treatment rooms including 2 spa suites	
DRINK	Asian Tea Lounge	
FEATURES	male and female saunas • steam rooms and ice fountain • indoor pool • sun terrace • gym • spa boutique • gift certificates	
NEARBY	Star Ferry • Cultural Centre • Museum of Art • Space Museum • Museum of History	
CONTACT	The Peninsula Spa by ESPA, Salisbury Road, Kowloon, Hong Kong • telephone: +852.2315 3322 • facsimile: +852.2315 3325 • email: spaphk@peninsula.com • website: www.peninsula.com	

PHOTOGRAPHS COURTESY OF THE PENINSULA SPA BY ESPA.

Hutong

In Hong Kong, the closest you can get to traditional Chinese courtyard houses commonly found in Peking's fast disappearing hutongs (ancient valleys or lanes) is, surprisingly, not along Hong Kong's own narrow streets but on the 28th floor of the ultra-modern high-rise, One Peking Road, in Tsim Sha Tsui.

Hutong has successfully recreated the historical charm reminiscent of such old courtyard houses, with its dramatic and post-modern décor set against a backdrop of Hong Kong Island's gleaming cityscape

through full-length windows. The juxtaposition of the traditional and the contemporary is what sets Hutong apart.

The ornate circular entranceway sets the enchanting mood as guests walk into the main dining area. Beautifully carved antique wooden screens and rustic tables add to the traditional appeal of the restaurant while red lanterns and night candles lend a soft, sensual tone to the muted, minimalist feel of the cement walls and wooden floors. Larger-than-life bamboo birdcages, silk curtains and cushions, as

THIS PAGE (FROM TOP): An eclectic mix of nostalgic Chinese items adds to the traditional feel of the restaurant; a dramatic contrast of the warm, classic interior with the cool, glittering cityscape outside.
OPPOSITE (FROM LEFT): The ornately carved circular entranceway framing the main dining area; the cement walls and wooden furniture create a cosy ambience together.

The juxtaposition of the traditional and the contemporary is what sets Hutong apart.

well as black ceramic plates and bowls create an interesting texture to the interiors.

Specialising in northern Chinese cuisine with some fiery influences from Sichuan Province, chef-cum-designer Calvin Yeung adds innovative flavours and cooking methods to traditional Peking dishes. Some of the restaurant's sought-after dishes include crispy lamb ribs coated with tantalising spices and served on a long wooden platter, bamboo clams steeped in Chinese wine and chilli padi, crunchy soft shell crabs made with Szechun red peppers, and spicy soup noodles flavoured by minced pork and

peanut sauce. In 2005, Hutong became the only Hong Kong restaurant to be featured on the *Conde Nast Traveller*'s 'Hot Tables' List for its stunning setting and fantastic food.

Owners Calvin—who shot to fame in 2000 with his first solo venture, an exquisite Chinese restaurant called Shui Hu Ju—and David Yeo are both prominent figures in Hong Kong's dining scene. The formidable pair now owns six of the city's most respected and raved-about restaurants.

Upstairs to Hutong, Aqua presents Italian and Japanese cuisine in one dynamic, stylish setting. Located in Festival Walk, the mall above Kowloon Tong Station, Thai restaurant Ayuthaiya emulates a sophisticated atmosphere lifted by pink backlit walls. At Times Square in Causeway Bay, Wasabisabi offers a contemporary environment for fresh, zingy Japanese cuisine while the nearby Water Margin wraps itself in traditional charm and ambience; and is perhaps the closest relative to Hutong itself.

FACTS

SEATS	200
FOOD	contemporary northern Chinese
DRINK	extensive wine list • cocktails • Chinese signature drinks
FEATURES	panoramic views of Hong Kong harbour • fine dining • private dining rooms
NEARBY	Star Ferry • Hong Kong Cultural Centre
CONTACT	28/F, One Peking Road, Tsim Sha Tsui, Hong Kong • telephone +852.3428 8342 • facsimile: +852. 3428 8484 • email: info@aqua.com.hk • website: www.aqua.com.hk

PHOTOGRAPHS COURTESY OF AQUA GROUP.

Harbour City

HARBOUR CITY 海港城

THIS PAGE: *Grand entrance of Harbour City.*

OPPOSITE: *Luxury brands and international labels draw in the wealthy shoppers and fashion-conscious to Harbour City.*

Tsim Sha Tsui is often considered the heart and soul of Hong Kong. A little rougher around the edges than other districts, many people find the bright neon lights, busy streets and boisterous street hawkers more akin to the pre-conceived notion of this diverse city. With numerous local restaurants and lively markets, there is a colourful, local atmosphere here that is sometimes lost among other modern developments elsewhere. With the highest concentration of museums—including Hong Kong Museum of Art, Museum of History and Space Museum—and some of the city's most spectacular views overlooking the iconic skyscrapers and The Peak of

Hong Kong Island, it is a must-see destination for any visitor. However it is often the shopping malls, numerous flagship stores and local boutiques that prove to be the most popular attractions. Indeed, Tsim Sha Tsui is one of the most famous shopping districts in Hong Kong. Nathan Road, its main thoroughfare, is referred to as the 'Golden Mile' for the multitude of shops that horde each side of the street for more than a mile. Canton Road, running parallel to Nathan Road, offers the more upmarket alternative synonymous with Hong Kong's glamorous reputation. Drawing a number of exclusive department stores and enticing high-end brands to open their flagship stores here, such as Louis Vuitton, Coach, Prada and Yves Saint Laurent, Canton Road is fast becoming an alluring shopping haven.

Harbour City is built on the original site of the shipping and cargo docks; it sits next to the Star Ferry pier and looks out

across Victoria Harbour to the Central District on Hong Kong Island. Being the largest shopping mall in Hong Kong, it covers a massive area of over 185,000 sq m (2 million sq ft), and contains more than 700 shops, over 50 restaurants, three hotels and two cinemas—undoubtedly an

impressive one-stop shopping and entertainment complex. Harbour City houses brands by a list of celebrity designers including Ralph Lauren, Vivienne Westwood and Louis Vuitton as well as those by local personalities such as Vivienne Tam and Lu Lu Cheng. Fashion labels such as Diesel , Miss Sixty, agnès b. and Zara draw in the hip and trendy shopping crowd. Lane Crawford, which has three other stores across Hong Kong, dominates a 7,500-sq-m (80,000-sq-ft) space and adds to the diverse array of designers in Harbour City. With cult-status bags, swanky shoes and every accessory you can imagine, this is the place for

finding the perfect outfit for any occasion. The gleaming white beauty department has over 160 different brands of cosmetics and beauty products, among them Chanel, Joyce Beauty, Kiehl's, La Prairie, Mary Quant and shu uemura. With the Aveda Lifestyle Hair Salon and Day Spa catering to tired and weary shoppers, shopping here can only be a pleasurable and therapeutic affair.

The ultimate crowd-puller of Harbour City is its sports section, which has become a well-known and well-loved landmark in Kowloon. While ladies contentedly browse through the numerous boutiques spread across the mall, men can also indulge in a little shopping with the huge variety of sporting goods available at SportX. The store tempts with Gigasports Super Store, Body Glove, Head, New Balance, Open and Callaway Golf Apparel, just to name a few of the famous brands on offer. You can pick up the latest pair of Birkenstocks, shop for accessories at Harley Davidson and keep up to date with the latest surf gear at Patagonia. Adding to the fun and sporty feel of SportX, there is a half-sized basketball court, rock-climbing playground and mini-golf putting area to pump up the shoppers' adrenaline.

A mega mall is not complete without a kids section, and yes, Harbour City has a whole floor called KidX—filled with cartoon

characters, model cars and apparel—just for the little ones. Armani Junior, DKNY Kids, Moch, Hysteric Mini, Elle Petite and United Colours of Benetton showcase their latest season's collections here. Don't forget Harbour City has the largest Toys 'R' Us in Asia as well. It is the city's top hangout for up-and-coming fashionistas and their mothers.

Not limited to fashion, beauty and sports, Harbour City is also a reliable source for electronic products. Well-known brands like B&O and Sony have stores here while Fortress and Broadway are among 20 electrical outlets which stock a wide range of the latest gadgets, making Harbour City a great place to compare

THIS PAGE (CLOCKWISE FROM TOP): **Get sporty at SportX; KidX is a kids paradise with a whole floor dedicated to the little ones; beauty products galore.**
OPPOSITE: **Harbour City is a mecca for shoppaholics.**

When you finally need a break from shopping in a maze of clothes, jewellery, sports and electronics shops, take your pick from over 50 restaurants at Harbour City. Offering cuisines from around the world, you can eat to your heart's content. From a casual bite at the California Pizza Kitchen to fine dining and a taste of Cantonese at the glamorous yè shanghai, you can indulge in all kinds of gastronomic delights at the mall. On the ground floor overlooking the Star Ferry terminal and the constant boat traffic along Victoria Harbour, the peaceful and nautical tones at Habitu the Pier and The Quarterdeck Kowloon make for a wonderful resting spot in your day of shopping.

quality and prices across all the top-range retailers. Another plus point that customers will appreciate is the global warranties on products that the stores here offer. It gives shoppers, especially tourists, a peace of mind and the necessary assurance.

...a dynamic spread of boutiques, international brands and specialised stores...

Throughout the year, Harbour City actively celebrates both international and local festivals; and it is a popular place to catch all kinds of live events—from firework displays and dragon dancing to Christmas Carols and Chinese New Year ceremonies. Every weekend, a 'Music in the City' event attracts a large crowd supporting local singers and songwriters. The Mall also hosts many of the luxury beauty road shows and car shows.

With such a dynamic spread of boutiques, international brands and specialised stores Harbour City remains the most popular, and certainly the largest mall in Hong Kong. A shopping paradise in its own right, this is the one place where you can find everything from a memory chip for your camera and the latest computer gadget to Furla's latest range of sexy bags and Prada shades—truly a shopping complex for everyone.

THIS PAGE: Enjoy great food and a view at Habitu the Pier; exquisite dining with dazzling city lights at The Quarterdeck Kowloon.

OPPOSITE (FROM TOP): Find premier brands of home entertainment systems at the mall; a stunning bird's-eye view of Harbour City by the Star Ferry.

PRODUCTS	fashion • accessories • sportswear • beauty products • children's toys and clothes • electrical goods
FEATURES	2 cinemas • over 50 restaurants • all-catering shopping complex
NEARBY	Kowloon • Hong Kong Museum of Art • Hong Kong Museum of History • Star Ferry
CONTACT	Harbour City, 3–27 Canton Road, Tsim Sha Tsui, Kowloon, Hong Kong • telephone: +852.2118 8666 • website: www.harbourcity.com.hk

PHOTOGRAPHS COURTESY OF HARBOUR CITY.

Heliservices

Famed for the mesmerising skyline of chrome and glass on Hong Kong Island, the million-dollar homes nestled into the steep slopes of The Peak, the sandy beaches of the outlying islands and the mountainous, rural New Territories, Hong Kong is a city best seen from the sky.

Flying at 460 m (1,500 ft) above a mass of skyscrapers is an exhilarating ride. With the International Finance Centre, Hong Kong's tallest building measuring over 400 m (1,300 ft), you will feel

dwarfed by the gargantuan towers of Hong Kong Island. And yet within moments, you are flying over another side of Hong Kong, rugged and rural with dramatic coastlines framing the outlying islands and local farmlands dotted among the New Territories. There are few cities that could offer such stunning diversity in one short helicopter ride.

Taking off from the roof of The Peninsula Hong Kong for a guided trip with your personal pilot may seem the ultimate sightseeing tour but Heliservices also provides a range of different packages. For an idyllic day out take an aerial tour of the Country Park and Sai Kung before landing on the beautiful Tap Mun Island for a leisurely lunch at Loi Lam's Seafood Restaurant and a wander around the local fishing village and nearby Tin Hau Temple. You are then swept back to The Peninsula in

There are few cities that could offer such stunning diversity in one short helicopter ride.

chat with the pilot and the other passengers. For longer distances Metrojet, Heliservices' sister company, is Hong Kong's only fully licensed business jet operator and can fly you anywhere in Asia. So whether you are flying down for a game of golf in Phuket or a dinner in Shanghai, Metrojet will ensure your grand

arrival through VIP channels. However, if glamorous is not your cup of tea, think action-packed adventure movies— Angelina Jolie's stunt double jumped from a Heliservices' helicopter in *Tomb Raider II*. You may not be Lara Croft, but for 5 minutes you can certainly let your imagination take flight.

time for a cocktail at sundown. For an evening of immeasurable style, Heliservices also offers a fly-and-dine package with The Peninsula Hong Kong where, after soaring above the city's sky-rises and the magnificent light show that befalls Victoria Harbour at dusk, you return to the hotel for a romantic dinner at the Philippe Starck-designed Felix or any of its other renowned restaurants.

Flying twin engine Squirrel helicopters, there is enough room for five people; each with an individual head set so you can

FACTS

PRODUCTS	helicopter sightseeing tours • business jet
FEATURES	5-seater helicopters • fly-and-dine packages • day-trips
NEARBY	everything
CONTACT	telephone: +852.2802 0200 • facsimile: +852.2824 2033 • email: chp@heliservices.com.hk • website: www.heliservices.com.hk

PHOTOGRAPHS COURTESY OF HELISERVICES.

Lane Crawford Canton Road

Established since 1850, Lane Crawford is still the leading fashion brand in a city famed for its glamorous shopping experiences. Competing alongside state-of-the-art shopping malls and standalone boutiques, Lane Crawford has effortlessly risen to the top of the pack with its eye-catching interiors and diverse range of products and services.

Keeping up with Hong Kong's regular makeovers, Lane Crawford has progressed and expanded rapidly to ensure its place in the latest, most fashionable districts. Tsim Sha Tsui in Kowloon, famed for its shopping, is a centre for local shops and international boutiques alike. Its busy streets are constantly packed with tourists and locals bargaining for clothes, gadgets and even food.

Harbour City, opposite the Star Ferry pier, is home to a range of elite brands. Its high-tech atmosphere and gleaming surroundings are perfect for a store such as Lane Crawford, which prides itself on aesthetics as much as fashion.

With impressive sculptures, bright lighting and avant-garde displays, Lane Crawford is a gallery of design. Each of its

...the largest home and lifestyle department...

four stores has a unique identity. Lane Crawford Canton Road in Harbour City houses the largest selection in men's designer fashion.

With Armani, Paul Smith, Hugo Boss, Adidas and more, all showcasing their latest designs, this is a playground for boys. Of course, girls too can join in the fun in the women's section, browsing through lingerie, shoes, handbags and contemporary designer fashion such as Chloé, Stella McCartney, Lanvin and Jimmy Choo. The Canton Road store also boasts

the largest home and lifestyle department filled with great gift ideas and contemporary designer furniture. Photo frames and lamps are displayed on beautifully decorated shelves. Steel bathtubs are filled with deluxe towels and bathrobes. Sleek sofas are surrounded by luxurious rugs.

With such an assorted range of products available, the temptations are great; and with complimentary home delivery amongst its many superior services, it is hard to leave Lane Crawford Canton Road empty-handed.

THIS PAGE (FROM LEFT): Chic women's apparel on display; sporty and casual men's wear.

OPPOSITE (FROM TOP): A huge section on men's shoes; luminous cosmetics counters; showcasing the largest home and lifestyle range among the other Lane Crawford stores.

FACTS

PRODUCTS	men's and women's fashion • beauty • shoes and accessories • fine jewellery • home and lifestyle
FEATURES	personal styling • complimentary home delivery • concierge service
NEARBY	Harbour City • Kowloon • Star Ferry
CONTACT	Lane Crawford, 3 Canton Road, Tsim Sha Tsui, Kowloon, Hong Kong • telephone +852.2118 3428 • facsimile: +852.2118 3448 • email: customerrelationship@lanecrawford.com • website: www.lanecrawford.com

PHOTOGRAPHS COURTESY OF LANE CRAWFORD.

The Peninsula Arcade

The Peninsula is one of very few heritage sites to have survived Hong Kong's stampede into the 21st century. Its colonial architecture, colourful history and reputation as one of the finest hotels in the world have ensured its long-standing position at the forefront of Hong Kong's star-studded scene, attracting as many celebrities now as it did over 75 years ago. Underneath the guest rooms that once accommodated Clark Gable and Charlie Chaplin, and the renowned restaurants, The Peninsula is also home to one of Asia's most prestigious shopping malls, The Peninsula Arcade.

Comprising over 80 shops and boutiques on the basement, ground and mezzanine floors of the hotel, The Peninsula Shopping Arcade includes the best of fashion and tailoring, jewellery, leather goods and accessories. Far removed from the neighbouring stalls along Nathan

THIS PAGE (FROM TOP): The Peninsula Boutique where you will find the most decadent chocolate; away from the bustling street markets, the side entrance to the arcade sets this shopping centre apart from the rest.

OPPOSITE (FROM LEFT): Original details of this grand old lady; Old-World charm and excellent service makes the Peninsula Arcade the ultimate choice for some high-class shopping.

THE PENINSULA ARCADE

...a serene and satisfying shopping experience.

Road's 'Golden Mile', The Peninsula Arcade provides a serene and satisfying shopping experience.

International brands of equal recognition to The Peninsula are showcased with designers including Dior, Chanel, Hermès, Louis Vuitton, Prada, Versace, Vivienne Tam and Ralph Lauren. Local prominence includes collections and vibrant designs from Shanghai Tang. For the ultimate night out in Hong Kong you will find the season's most glamorous outfit and accessories all under the roof of The Peninsula. And with Bvlgari, Cartier, Piaget and Tiffany & Co. in the arcade, the glittering final touches are just a quick detour in your shopping trip.

The Peninsula Boutique is also located in the Arcade offering a myriad of upmarket souvenirs and gifts, including 'Simply Peninsula' pampering body care products and 'Naturally Peninsula' organic food lines. Most importantly, it's here you will find The Peninsula's renowned chocolates, champagnes, pastries and Chinese teas.

After browsing through the world's most exclusive brands The Peninsula offers a glamorous reprieve with afternoon tea in the stunning colonial setting of The Lobby. And, if a refreshing cup of earl grey is not enough to soothe the weight of your heavy bags, a trip to The Peninsula Spa is guaranteed to make your body and mind feel as clear and sparkling as a diamond.

FACTS

PRODUCTS	exclusive international brands • clothing • jewellery • watches • leather goods • local designers • haute couture
FOOD	Gaddi's: French • Felix: contemporary • The Verandah: Mediterranean • Chesa: Swiss • Spring Moon: Cantonese • Imasa: Japanese • Pool Terrace • The Lobby: afternoon tea
DRINK	The Lobby • The Bar • Felix
FEATURES	tailoring • limousine service
NEARBY	Star Ferry • Cultural Centre • Museum of Art • Space Museum • Museum of History
CONTACT	The Peninsula Hong Kong, Salisbury Road, Kowloon, Hong Kong • telephone: +852.2920 2888 • facsimile: +852.2722 4170 • email: phk@peninsula.com • website: www.peninsula.com

PHOTOGRAPHS COURTESY OF THE PENINSULA ARCADE.

index

Numbers in *italics* denote pages where pictures appear.
Numbers in **bold** denote map pages.

index

picturecredits + acknowledgements

The publisher would like to thank the following for permission to reproduce their photographs:

1/5 55 (below)
Ahmat; Edmond Tse 47 (left)
Alan Clements back cover: reflection of an old housing estate, 21, 62 (left)
Alex Lau 20 (below), 39 (right)
Alex Woo 53 (top left), 161 (top left), 174 (top)
Anson Ki 38 (top)
Astor Shek back cover: lantern exhibit details, 43 (top)
Bernard Tse 8–9
Bjørn Smestad 175 (below)
Bobby Yip/Reuters 26 (top), 171
Bono Tsang 51 (top left)
Caveman Lee (www.pbase.com/caveman_lee) 18
Che Francisco 163 (below)
Chopstix Media front cover: siew mai, 50 (top)
Chris Lee 33 (top)
Catabell C. Y. Lee 43 (below), 63 (below)
Codino Divino 28 (below), 179
Crosswell Collins 64 (top)
Dallas Stribley/Lonely Planet 22 (top)
Dallas Stribley/Getty 6
David Serra 44 (below), 45 (top), 57 (left), 58, 156 (below), 162, 169 (below), 172
Diane Lee 54 (below)
Dindin Lagdameo 66 (top), 176 (below right)
Eneko Ametzaga 63 (top)

Eva Angermann 42 (below)
Evyns Chan 175 (top)
Four Seasons Hotel Hong Kong back cover: ice fountain at the sauna
Framewerkz back cover: rock concert, 4, 20 (top), 42 (top), 48 (top), 49 (right), 56 (below), 61 (below), 152, 160, 167 (right), 170 (left), 173 (below), 177
FINDS; Framewerkz 49 (top left)
George Lin 54 (top)
Glenn Carter 167 (left)
Glenn Michael Tan front cover: Mickey Mouse details, 28 (top)
Graham Uden 14 (left), 17, 45 (below), 56 (top)
James Marshall/Corbis 154, 155 (top)
Jean Kugler/Getty 22 (below)
Jim Erickson/Corbis 170 (right)
Jim Shortall/IronCatastrophe.com 163 (top)
Jörg Sundermann front cover: neon street lights, traffic light, the bar at Felix, view from The Peak, front cover flap: furniture detail at boutique, 2, 5, 12, 14 (right), 23 (left), 29, 30, 32, 33 (below), 34 (top and below), 35 (top), 36 (below), 37, 50 (below), 55 (top), 57 (right), 65 (top and below), 68 (top), 202–203
Keven Law back cover flap: dragonfly, 155 (below)
Kevin Phillips 13 (top), 16 (below), 23 (right), 25 (right), 26 (below), 61 (top), 161 (below)
Kin Cheung/Reuters 27
Kou front cover flap: showroom
Lane Crawford ifc mall back cover flap: CD bar
Leif Tobias 67 (right)
Linda K. Robinson 59 (below)
Lisa Damayanti 156 (top right)

Lynn Chen 38 (below), 51 (right), 53 (top)
Maciej Dakowicz 13 (below), 52, 59 (top), 67 (top left), 178 (below)
Marc Charnal 159 (top and below)
Michael Hansen 157
Michael Reynolds/Corbis 24
Michael S. Yamashita/Corbis 69
Michel Setboun/Getty 19
Monica Hong 44 (top)
Neil MacLean 16 (left)
OVO back cover: showroom
Paul Myers (paulmyers@postmaster.co.uk) front cover flap: Bruce Lee art installation, artwork and photo 46
Peter Kwok 48 (below)
Phil Weymouth/Lonely Planet 40 (below)
Ricci Wong 41
Rickly Wong 60
Roderick Kar 173 (top)
Royalty-free/Corbis 68 (below)
Shanghai Tang back cover: product details
Tam Hin Lun front cover: Joyce fashion show, 15, 35 (below), 39 (left), 40 (top), 47 (right), 53 (below), 66 (below), 166 (below)
The Hong Kong Jockey Club 169 (top)
The Peninsula Hong Kong 36 (top left and right)
The Peninsula Spa by ESPA front cover: spa details
Wally McNamee/Corbis 25 (top left)
William Furniss back cover: dragon boat, bun tower, 62 (right), 156 (top left), 158, 164 (top and below), 165, 166 (top), 168, 178 (top)
Yvonne 64 (below)
Zoë Jaques 174 (below), 176 (top and below left)

directory

hotels

Conrad Hong Kong (page 70)
Pacific Place, 88 Queensway
telephone : +852.2521 3838
facsimile : +852.2521 3888
hongkonginfo@conradhotels.com
www.ConradHotels.com

Four Seasons Hotel Hong Kong (page 74)
8 Finance Street, Central
telephone : +852.319.688 88
facsimile : +852.231.968 899
www.fourseasons.com/hongkong

Grand Hyatt Hong Kong (page 80)
1 Harbour Road, Wan Chai
telephone : +852.2588 1234
facsimile : +852.2802 0677
info.ghhk@grandhyatt.com.hk
www.hongkong.grand.hyatt.com

J W Marriot Hotel Hong Kong (page 82)
Pacific Place, 88 Queensway
telephone : +852.2810 8366
facsimile : +852.2845 0737
hotel@marriott.com.hk
www.marriott.com/HKGDT

Langham Place Hotel (page 180)
555 Shanghai Street, Mong Kok, Kowloon
telephone : +852.3552 3388
facsimile : +852.3552 3322
hkg.lph.info@langhamhotels.com
hongkong.langhamplacehotels.com

Le Méridien Cyberport (page 84)
100 Cyberport Road
telephone : +852.2980 7788
facsimile : +852.2980 7888
welcome@lemeridien-cyberport.com
www.lemeridien/hongkong

Shama (page 90)
8F Wyndham Place,
44 Wyndham Street, Central
telephone : +852.2522 3082
facsimile : +852.2522 2762
info@shama.com
www.shama.com

The Peninsula Hong Kong (page 182)
Salisbury Road, Kowloon
telephone : +852.2920 2888
facsimile : +852.2722 4170
phk@peninsula.com
www.peninsula.com

The Ritz-Carlton, Hong Kong (page 88)
3 Connaught Road, Central
telephone : +852.2877 6666
facsimile : +852.2877 6778
info@ritz-carlton-hk.com
www.ritzcarlton.com

spas

Chuan Spa (page 184)
Langham Place Hotel, Level 41,
555 Shanghai Street, Mong Kok, Kowloon
telephone : +852.3552 3510
facsimile : +852.3552 3529
hkg.lph.info@chuanspa.com
www.chuanspa.com

Plateau Spa (page 92)
Grand Hyatt Hong Kong
1 Harbour Road, Wan Chai
telephone : +852.2584 7688
facsimile : +852.2584 7738
plateau.ghhk@hyattintl.com
www.plateau.com.hk

The Peninsula Spa by ESPA (page 186)
The Peninsula Hong Kong
Salisbury Road, Kowloon
telephone : +852.2315 3322
facsimile : +852.2315 3325
spaphk@peninsula.com
www.peninsula.com

restaurants

1/5 (page 94)
9 Star Street, Wan Chai
telephone : +852.2520 2515
facsimile : +852.2596 0283
1/5@elite-concepts.com
www.elite-concepts.com

Cinecittà (page 96)
9 Star Street, Wan Chai,
telephone : +852.2529 0199
facsimile : +852.2529 5399
cin@elite-concepts.com
www.elite-concepts.com

FINDS (page 98)
2nd Floor LKF Tower,
33 Wyndham Street, Central
telephone : +852.2522 9318
facsimile : +852.2521 9818
reservations@finds.com.hk
www.finds.com.hk

Hutong (page 188)
28/F, One Peking Road,
Tsim Sha Tsui, Kowloon
telephone : +852.3428 8342
facsimile : +852.3428 8484
info@aqua.com.hk
www.aqua.com.hk

JJ's (page 100)
Grand Hyatt Hong Kong
1 Harbour Road, Wan Chai
telephone : +852.2584 7662
facsimile : +852.2824 2060
jjs.ghhk@hyattintl.com
hongkong.grand.hyatt.com

KEE Club (page 102)
6th Floor, 32 Wellington Street, Central
telephone : +852.2810 9000
facsimile : +852.2868 0036
info@keeclub.com
www.keeclub.com

Lan Kwai Fong (page 104)
UG/F, California Tower, 30-32
D'Aguilar Street, Central
Lux:
telephone : +852.2868 9538
facsimile : +852.2869 9510
Café des Artistes:
telephone : +852.2526 3880
facsimile : +852.2147 3456

Kyoto Joe:
telephone : +852.2804 6800
facsimile : +852.2804 6030
info@lkfgroup.com
www.lkfe.com

Lotus Restaurant (page 106)
37–43 Pottinger Street, Central
telephone : +852.2543 6290
facsimile : +852.2541 6588
info@lotus.hk
www.lotus.hk

one fifth grill (page 108)
9 Star Street, Wan Chai
telephone : +852.2529 6038
facsimile : +852.2596 0283
ofg@elite-concepts.com
www.elite-concepts.com

One Harbour Road (page 110)
Grand Hyatt Hong Kong
1 Harbour Road, Wan Chai
telephone : +852.2584 7938
facsimile : +852.2824 2060
info.ghhk@hyattintl.com
www.hongkong.grand.hyatt.com

yé shanghai (page 112)
Hong Kong Island:
Pacific Place, Level 3, Pacific Place
telephone : +852.2918 9833
facsimile : +852.2918 0651
Kowloon:
6/F Marco Polo Hongkong Hotel
telephone : +852.2376 3322
facsimile : +852.2376 3189
ysk@elite-concepts.com
www.elite-concepts.com

shops

Barney Cheng (page 114)
bridal shop: 1 Duddell Street, Central
telephone : +852.2905 1011
facsimile : +852.3011 6248
celebration@barneycheng.com
studio : 12/F Worldwide Comm Bldg,
34 Wyndham Street, Central
telephone : +852.2530 2829
facsimile : +852.2530 2835
bureau@barneycheng.com
www.barneycheng.com

Carnet Jewellery (page 116)
shop : Shop 119, Prince's Building,
First Floor, 10 Chater House,
Central
telephone : +852.2805 0113
facsimile : +852.2805 0180
shop@carnetjewellery.com
office : Suite 505, Peter Building, 58
Queen's Road, Central
telephone : +852.2526 5194
facsimile : +852.2845 9276
carnet@carnetjewellery.com
www.carnetjewellery.com

Covatta Design (page 118)
telephone : +852.3118 7381
facsimile : +852.2525 5118
design@covatta.net
www.covattadesign.com

G.O.D. (page 120)
Leighton Centre, Sharp Street East,
Causeway Bay
telephone : +852.2890 5555
48, Hollywood Road, Central
telephone : +852.2805 1876
3/F Hong Kong Hotel, Harbour City,
Tsim Sha Tsui
telephone : +852.2784 5555
info@god.com.hk
www.god.com.hk

Kou (page 122)
22F Fung House, 19-20 Connaught Road,
Central
telephone : +852.2530 2234
facsimile : +852.2849 4771
info@kouconcept.com
www.kouconcept.com

Lane Crawford Canton Road (page 198)
3 Canton Road, Tsim Sha Tsui, Kowloon
telephone : +852.2118 3428
facsimile : +852.2118 3448
customerrelation@lanecrawford.com
www.lanecrawford.com

Lane Crawford ifc mall (page 124)
Podium 3, ifc mall, 8 Finance Street, Central
telephone : +852.2118 3388
facsimile : +852.2118 3389
customerrelationship@lanecrawford.com
www.lanecrawford.com

Lane Crawford Pacific Place (page 126)
Pacific Place, 88 Queensway, Admiralty
telephone : +852.2118 3668
facsimile : +852.2118 3669
customerrelationship@lanecrawford.com
www.lanecrawford.com

Lane Crawford Times Square (page 128)
Times Square, 1 Matheson Street,
Causeway Bay
telephone : +852.2118 3638
facsimile : +852.2118 3588
customerrelationship@lanecrawford.com
www.lanecrawford.com

OVO Home (page 130)
GF 16 Queen's Road East, Wan Chai
telephone : +852.2526 7226
facsimile : +852.2526 7227
info@ovo.com.hk
www.ovo.com.hk

OVO Garden (page 130)
GF 16 Wing Fung Street, Wan Chai
telephone : +852.2529 2599
facsimile : +852.2529 2569
info@ovogarden.com.hk
www.ovogarden.com.hk

Schoeni Art Gallery (page 138)
21–31 Old Bailey Street, Central
Branch Gallery: 27 Hollywood Road, Central
telephone : +852.2869 8802
facsimile : +852.2522 1528
gallery@schoeni.com.hk
www.schoeni.com.hk

Shanghai Tang (page 140)
Pedder Building, 12 Pedder Street, Central
telephone : +852.2537 2888
facsimile : +852.2156 9898
contactus@shanghaitang.com
www.shanghaitang.com

Sonjia (page 142)
2 Sun Street, Wan Chai
telephone : +852.2529 6223
facsimile : +852.2529 6328
info@sonjiaonline.com
www.sonjiaonline.com

Starstreet (page 144)
Wan Chai
info@starstreet.com.hk
www.starstreet.com.hk

Tayma Fine Jewellery (page 148)
Shop 252, 2nd Floor, Prince's Building,
10 Chater Road, Central
telephone : +852.2525 5280
facsimile : +852.2526 1017
finedesign@taymajewellery.com
www.taymajewellery.com

The Peninsula Arcade (page 200)
The Peninsula Hong Kong,
Salisbury Road, Kowloon
telephone : +852.2920 2888
facsimile : +852.2722 4170
phk@peninsula.com
www.peninsula.com

shopping malls

Harbour City (page 190)
3–27 Canton Road, Tsim Sha Tsui, Kowloon
telephone : +852.2118 8666
www.harbourcity.com.hk

Pacific Place (page 132)
88 Queensway
telephone : +852.2844 8988
ppshopping@swireproperties.com
www.pacificplace.com.hk

Times Square (page 150)
1 Matheson Street, Causeway Bay
telephone : +852.2118 8900
facsimile : +852.2118 8934
tselpro@timessquare.com.hk
www.timessquare.com.hk

helicopter services

Heliservices (page 196)
telephone : +852.2802 0200
facsimile : +852.2824 2033
chp@heliservices.com.hk
www.heliservices.com.hk